Communism in Vietnam

A DOCUMENTARY STUDY
of Theory, Strategy
and Operational Practices

RODGER SWEARINGEN and
HAMMOND ROLPH

3129500946 5138

American Bar Association
Standing Committee on
Education About Communism and
Contrast With Liberty Under Law

Library of Congress Catalog Card Number: 67—18823

THIRD PRINTING 1970

Copyright © 1967 by the American Bar Association
Rodger Swearingen and Hammond Rolph

PRICE $1.25

PRINTED IN THE UNITED STATES OF AMERICA

Table of Contents

IV

V

VI

VII

acknowledgements

The authors wish to extend their appreciation to the many individuals and organizations who have so materially assisted in the production of this book. A note of thanks is due to the agencies and officers of the Government of the Republic of Vietnam and the United States Government for their efforts on our behalf to obtain original documents of the Viet Cong movement. Student research assistants and Vietnamese translators at the Research Institute on Communist Strategy and Propaganda worked most diligently to translate certain of these documents from the original Vietnamese. The clerical staff of the Institute gave unstintingly of its time and energy to the typing and collation of the original manuscript.

We also wish to thank the American Bar Association's Standing Committee on Education About Communism and Its Contrast With Liberty Under Law for its generous support of this project, and especially to acknowledge the invaluable assistance of the Bar Association staff, which has been so very helpful and efficient in the technical preparation of the copy.

R.S.
H.M.R.

Preface to first printing

. . . North Vietnam has attacked the independent nation of South Vietnam. Its object is total conquest. . . . The confused nature of this conflict cannot mask the fact that it is the new face of an old enemy . . . the deepening shadow of Communist China.

President Lyndon B. Johnson
April 8, 1966

That the greatest nation on earth, America, has agreed to come as a member to offer her help to all the countries of Asia in planning and developing measures that will end the causes of war, and to encourage Asian initiative and to join all in the quest for peace is a tribute to American sincerity and a recognition of the validity of Asian aims. . . . What is at stake in Vietnam is not only the fate of one country but the future of Asia and the world.

Ferdinand E. Marcos
President of the Republic of
the Philippines
October 24, 1966

In 1962 the American Bar Association created what is now called the Standing Committee on Education About Communism and Its Contrast With Liberty Under Law. The Committee was organized on the premise that World Communism—through a continuum of propaganda, subversion, political warfare and "armed struggle"—puts into jeopardy the rule of law and the value system of individual freedoms embodied in the Constitution and the Bill of Rights.

Since its inception the Committee has supported three major

programs: (1) institutes and workshops for high school teachers on "Democracy vs. Communism"; (2) briefing sessions on national defense and international security affairs for lawyers and other professional groups; and (3) publication of analyses of current Communist intentions, goals, strategies, tactics and capabilities.

Education about the nature of Communist dogma and dictatorship—in contrast to liberty-under-law and democratic pluralism—is admittedly "controversial." It is precisely for that reason that it is imperative for responsible leadership to make certain that teachers are not faced with the dilemma of either (a) ignoring a vast subject so intimately connected with the fate of freedom everywhere, or (b) turning for assistance to unprofessional sources.

The Committee takes satisfaction in its five-year cooperative effort with scholars which has provided workshops and institutes —often for academic credit—for nearly 10,000 teachers from 45 states through: 30 college and university summer schools; in-service training in New York City, Atlanta, Houston and Miami; and educational television in four states. The Committee is equally gratified that its publications have been reviewed, abstracted or reprinted in some 440 newspapers with a combined circulation of 35 million, that two of its books have been translated into Spanish and circulated widely abroad, that one of its publications was distributed to 7,000 high schools in 20 states for the use of students debating foreign policy issues, and that its work has been commended by former Presidents Harry S. Truman and Dwight D. Eisenhower as well as Mr. J. Edgar Hoover and the Honorable Allen W. Dulles.

Its publications include the following paperback books: *The New Czars vs. The Rule of Law* (1964); *Peaceful Coexistence: A Communist Blueprint for Victory* by Richard V. Allen (1964); *Democracy Confronts Communism in World Affairs* by Richard L. Walker (1965); *Peace or Peaceful Coexistence?* by Richard V. Allen (1966); and *The China Danger* by Richard L.

Walker (1966). It also published three lectures delivered to the Graduate School of Business Administration, Harvard University, by Mr. William C. Sullivan under the title of ". . . *Freedom Is The Exception*" (1965).

In furtherance of its policy of making available to the public objective analyses of Communist strategies—based on such primary sources as official Communist journals, radio broadcasts from Peking and Moscow, statements and books by Party leaders and formal resolutions adopted at conferences—the Committee commissioned Dr. Rodger Swearingen to undertake this study of the goals, methods and interests of Moscow, Peking, Hanoi and the Viet Cong as those relate to Communist aggression against South Vietnam. Dr. Swearingen is the Director, Research Institute on Communist Strategy and Propaganda, University of Southern California, and he was joined in this work by his colleague at the Institute, Commander Hammond Rolph, USN (Ret).

This book is a factual uncovering of the nature of "modern" aggression through agitation, terror, subversion, guerrilla war and the use of proxies to confuse world public opinion. It is crucial to the future of freedom that the court of world opinion be guided by facts rather than superficial slogans, by the weight of evidence, not the length of the picket line.

This book is not intended as a policy statement of the American Bar Association.

STANDING COMMITTEE ON EDUCATION ABOUT
COMMUNISM AND ITS CONTRAST WITH
LIBERTY UNDER LAW

July 1967

Note to Third Printing

Continuing requests for "Communism in Vietnam" have prompted the Committee to reprint this book.

February 1970

Standing Committee on Education About Communism and its Contrast with Liberty Under Law.

I

Introduction

This study of Communist strategy and propaganda in Vietnam does not deal with United States policy. It is concerned with the enemy we face—his unconventional doctrines of war, his emphasis on "liberation," guerrilla warfare, propaganda, subversion, and terror. This is a new kind of challenge, and it would be well to recognize that fact at the outset. It can be argued that the struggle in Vietnam represents a test not only of the Communist strategy and tactics of "national liberation" war, but also of the will and imagination which the United States and its allies are prepared to devote to meeting that challenge. Southeast Asia is the major world area in which Communist expansionist strategy has not been effectively contained. While there is no guarantee that success in checking it will produce a situation of quiet containment such as Europe enjoys, the momentum of Asian Communism would undoubtedly be blunted by its failure in Vietnam.

Conflict in Vietnam did not, of course, begin yesterday. Some Americans may not realize that the struggle long antedates United States involvement in it and that the Vietnamese have been undergoing an ordeal of violence and facing an uncertain future for a generation. Other Americans who are aware of this fact see it as a transcending reason for terminating hostilities quickly, regardless of the price. The first group frequently fails to see the complexities arising from a quarter-century of

Vietnamese internal strife, while the latter is reluctant to acknowledge the political, economic, social and strategic consequences of Communist victory. Although an end to the fighting would appear highly desirable to many, both Vietnamese and foreign, a "peace settlement" would scarcely resolve the basic issues in Vietnam or prevent the Vietnamese Communists from continuing the struggle on a political and subversive level in a manner which would seriously jeopardize the future of South Vietnam.

Vietnam is unique among postwar Southeast Asian nations by virtue of Communist dominance of its road to freedom from western rule and the role Communism has played in the subsequent painful process of nation-building. The historical record clearly shows that from the outset of the present violent era, and even before, the commanding elements in nationalist and independence movements in Vietnam were Marxist-Leninists. Communists controlled the independence war against the French, and it is they who guide the present conflict in South Vietnam, which they label "the continuing struggle for freedom and independence."

To be sure, there has been over the years non-Communist nationalist leadership in Vietnam. There were, in fact, many nationalists of note who contributed to the patriotic cause of independence. However, they were largely divided and ineffectual, generally no match for their Marxist competitors. The one great exception was Ngo Dinh Diem, who as an authentic nationalist built the state of South Vietnam in the aftermath of the Geneva Accords. However, since his role was largely played in the post-independence phase and as he had not been a major figure in the anti-colonial war, Diem never successfully refuted the Communists' credentials as the nationalist "vanguard." This was true despite the fairly widespread knowledge of the social consequences of Communist control in North Vietnam.

Ever since its beginnings as an organized movement, Vietnamese Communism has been distinguished by an extraordinary continuity of leadership, an exceptional ability to outmaneuver and submerge its rivals, a noteworthy flexibility in tactical approaches to unswerving strategic goals, and a remarkable ability to communicate to the Vietnamese people in terms of nationalism as well as Marxism.

The leadership cadre which developed around Ho Chi Minh prior to and after the founding of the Indochina Communist Party in 1930 is probably the longest uninterrupted directorate in world Communism. In the light of events in China since early 1966, it can now certainly lay claim to being the most cohesive. For in spite of the known and suspected differences over ideology and tactics within this inner circle, these men have shown a notable discipline in working together for common goals. Ho can indeed claim today to be almost the only "old Bolshevik" remaining in a key power position in a Communist state.

Following his early work in the first half of the 1920's in the French Communist Party, in Moscow, and as a Comintern agent for the Far East, Ho Chi Minh, then known as Nguyen Ai Quoc, moved on to the specific task of developing the Vietnamese independence movement. He showed his great abilities in organization and maneuver at this stage with the founding of a crypto-Communist organization known as the Vietnam Revolutionary Youth League in 1925. This League was organized in Canton as a rallying point for revolutionary nationalist expatriates. Ho's operations until the 1940's were entirely outside his native country, but this apparently in no way diminished his stature as a nationalist leader as compared to those who remained in Vietnam to face persecution by the French colonial authorities. It was during the period after 1925 that Ho began to gather around him some of the devoted key associates who remain with him to this day, such as Pham Van Dong, now Premier of North Vietnam.

By 1930, Ho had succeeded, with Moscow's assistance and the help of Comintern pressure, in welding three squabbling Marxist groups into a unified Indochina Communist Party (ICP), and as his organization burgeoned, the capacity of the Stalinist core to undercut, neutralize, isolate or even destroy both rival groups and untrustworthy cohorts became apparent. Ho's party assiduously promoted the growth of Marxist influence while carefully making an effective appeal to Vietnamese national sentiment. His strategy involved the envelopment and submergence of non-Communist nationalist personalities and groups, pre-emption of their political ground by more clever articulation of program and more energetic execution of policy, and from time to time assassination or the exposure of such rivals to the colonial police. The factor of good fortune should also not be overlooked. One of the strongest and most vigorous of the rival non-Communist groups not directly linked to Ho— the Vietnam Nationalist Party—was crushed by the French after an abortive uprising attempted by that party in 1930, and it remained moribund for more than a decade. Cadres of the new ICP profited greatly in the period following this fiasco, although Communist historians deny that the repression of the uprising was anything but a disaster for the cause of independence.

The flexibility of the ICP was such that neither setbacks within Vietnam, acute differences among Vietnamese revolutionaries nor the tortuous course of Kremlin policy ever destroyed the Party's effectiveness as a political movement. It survived French reprisals for the ICP-inspired strikes and uprisings in 1930 and 1931, as well as the vigorous French anti-Communist campaigns of 1939-42. During much of this time the ICP also overcame a threat from an increasingly strong Trotskyist movement in Vietnam and even succeeded in using this hated "deviationist" group to good advantage in limited local electoral cooperation. Somehow the expatriate leadership managed to maintain direction of the hard-pressed and sometimes bewildered apparatus within the country. The success of the Vietnamese Communists in the hard school of experience in the 1930's established the ICP as pre-eminent in the leadership of Vietnamese revolutionary nationalism.

Ever responsive to shifts in Moscow's line, Vietnamese Communism adjusted itself, however painfully, to a series of Comintern zigs and zags. First there was Stalin's policy of Communist cooperation with the bourgeois Chinese Nationalists during 1924-27 and the ignominious fiasco which followed; then the Popular Front period of "cooperation" with the French in the mid-1930's; the Hitler-Stalin pact period of 1939-41; and the swift transformation of World War II from an "imperialist" to an "anti-imperialist" war after the German invasion of Russia. At the same time, however, Ho was laying the groundwork for the stronger and more independent position he would develop within Vietnam during and after World War II, a posture which would enable him to pursue with greater autonomy his goals of overthrowing French rule, unification of Vietnam, and ultimately socialist "transformation" of the entire country.

One element of Vietnamese Communist doctrine which embraces the movement's continuity, flexibility, dominance of rivals and unswerving attention to ultimate objectives is the striking blend of nationalism and Marxism achieved by Ho Chi Minh and his entourage. The most evident organizational expression of this mix has been the use of the machinery of the "united front." Justification for this course of collaboration with non-Communist elements was formulated in the context of a two-stage theory of revolution in backward colonial areas: first, the "bourgeois democratic" stage of liberation from imperialist hegemony, then the second step involving socialist transformation of society. Ho Chi Minh assiduously practiced the politics of the first stage until 1954, joining with non-Communist nationalist groups and persons, using their talents for the common cause of promoting independence from France, neutralizing them as necessary, and isolating or destroying those who refused him complete obedience. Always the Communist Party remained the "vanguard" and leader of these fronts.

While such collaboration had been practiced earlier, Ho's most significant use of the united front technique was his organization in 1941 of a coalition of expatriate independence groups in southern China known as the Vietnam Independence League (the Viet Minh). This front, later greatly expanded in the wave of enthusiastic nationalism which followed World War II, was the vehicle which was used to defeat the French and bring Ho to power in North Vietnam. With the assistance of some Nationalist Chinese and United States agencies, the Viet Minh were able to return secretly to northern Vietnam during the Japanese occupation and to organize small guerrilla bands.

After the French administration was overthrown by the Japanese in March, 1945, the pace of Viet Minh development quickened, and by the time the Japanese collapsed later that year, the Communist-controlled Viet Minh quickly seized power in a large part of Vietnam and proclaimed the Democratic Republic of Vietnam. There followed a period of chaos and bloodshed—frequently marked by Viet Minh liquidation of Trotskyists and uncooperative nationalists—which set the stage for much of the personal bitterness and the spirit of political vendetta which characterize the Vietnam struggle to this day. While the Communists were establishing themselves in all key positions of power and leadership in the Viet Minh at that time and in the following months, Ho was careful to hold high the banner of nationalism and to present very mild social reform programs which would gain wide support, all in keeping with the stage of "bourgeois-democratic revolution." He even went so far as to make the gesture of dissolving the ICP, replacing it with a Marxist "study group."

As the French were in no position to return to Indochina immediately after World War II ended, the task of accepting the surrender of the Japanese and arranging for their repatriation was assigned to the Allied forces nearest at hand: the British based in the India-Burma theater and the Nationalist Chinese armies in south China, who occupied the southern and northern halves of Indochina respectively. Whatever the reason, neither of these forces seriously or effectively attempted to prevent the consolidation of Viet Minh control over much of Vietnam, although the Nationalist Chinese sponsored an ill-fated endeavor by a revived Vietnam Nationalist Party to establish itself in Tonkin. However, within a relatively short time, and with British and American acquiescence, the first elements of the French Expeditionary Corps arrived in the south to begin what would be a nine-year attempt to return Indo-China to French control.

In March 1946 Ho reached a short-lived *modus vivendi* with the French who appeared to recognize Vietnam's independence. It broke down in the following months as tensions rose over numerous incidents. In December 1946, following a French naval bombardment of Haiphong the previous month, the Viet Minh took to the field in open warfare against the colonial power.

As this first Vietnamese "people's war" got underway, Ho and his inner circle again moved skillfully on two fronts, on the one hand preparing and leading the anti-French resistance and on the other neutralizing or destroying those non-Communist leaders who rallied to the Viet Minh but did not acquiesce in total Marxist control of the movement. During the long struggle, the Viet Minh perfected the political, administrative and military organization in the countryside which would eventually produce a Communist state in North Vietnam. They reconstituted the Communist Party in 1951 as the Vietnamese Workers Party, or *Lao Dong,* and from that time onward there was no question as to the identity of the "vanguard" of the Vietnamese revolution.

Until 1949, Chinese Communism had little direct effect on events in Vietnam. Ho Chi Minh is a Moscow- and Comintern-trained leader; almost alone among Asian Communists in power, Ho has this bond with the original fountainhead of the world Communist movement. Although he also spent some time in the mid-1920's with the Chinese revolutionists, and is reported by some authorities to have been in Communist areas of north China in the period 1936-38, Ho and his movement have not been considered especially Maoist-oriented. After the Chinese Communist forces arrived at the Indochina border in 1949, however, Mao Tse-tung's political and military influence on the Vietnamese Communists began to grow. His doctrines of protracted "people's war" seemed quite applicable to the anti-French resistance. Moreover, the Communist conquest of China spelled doom for French efforts to contain the Viet Minh, for it provided a direct source of outside support so vital to the success of insurgent movements. Masses of Chinese weapons and supplies flowed across the border to the Viet Minh guerrillas, who were soon transformed into something more closely resembling a conventional army, which increasingly frustrated French military efforts. Finally the French, defeated perhaps as much by their own political ineffectiveness, strategic blundering, arrogance, tactical ineptitude and lack of support at home as by Viet Minh prowess, gave up the struggle and signed an armistice with the Communists.

The Geneva Agreement of 1954 which ended the anti-French war set the stage for the present struggle in Vietnam. It ended the first American commitment in Vietnam, which had consisted of material aid to the French, given in the vain hope that, while resisting the Viet Minh, they would make meaningful concessions to non-Communist Vietnamese nationalism. However, the agreement foreshadowed further serious United States involvement in that unhappy land. The Geneva document cut Vietnam in two, but unwholesome as such an arrangement was, it did allow an opportunity for almost half of the country's population to develop outside a Marxist totalitarian framework. What it crucially failed to provide was enforcement machinery which might have given some protection to the South against subversion, infiltration, and insurgency, inspired and supported from the North.

Although there was grumbling among the Viet Minh leadership over the "half a loaf" result at Geneva, Ho and his men may have counted on war-wracked South Vietnam to fall into their hands either through total political and economic collapse or by manipulating the 1956 unification elections called for in the Geneva Agreement's supplemental "political declaration." What they failed to foresee were the political acumen and authoritarian efficiency and vigor which President Ngo Dinh Diem would demonstrate in making the South a viable and thriving entity within four or five years after Geneva. Hanoi's frustration over the growing prosperity in South Vietnam was all the more accentuated by severe dislocations in the North arising from ruthless application of traditional Soviet developmental methods. North Vietnam withheld its hand for some time after Geneva, but finally was impelled, largely by the internal logic of its own doctrine of revolution *cum* nationalism, to move against Saigon. The present attempt to destroy the southern republic by whatever means feasible is thus a major piece of "unfinished business" along Ho's long revolutionary road, but his attempt to carry out this enterprise has serious implications not only for Vietnam but also for the stability and security of Southeast Asia, the success of U.S. foreign policy, and the future of the world Communist movement.

Much has been written on Vietnam concerning United States

policy, American losses, critics of American policy, the Saigon government and administration, and the plight of the Vietnamese themselves. There are few studies documenting and analyzing the strategy and tactics of the enemy, particularly in terms of all the major Communist actors in the Vietnam drama. The present volume is designed to be an introduction to this aspect of the war.

Specifically, this documentary study first reviews the development of the theory and strategy of "people's war" from Lenin to Lin Piao. This is followed by an analysis of Hanoi's role in the Vietnam war in terms of its military and political strategy as well as its stand on negotiations and such controversial matters as the critics of United States policy.

The next section of the study, "The Viet Cong: Politics at Gunpoint," takes up systematically the often misconstrued nature of the insurgent movement and includes considerable previously unpublished documentary material secured in Vietnam. Critical topics include organization and leadership of the National Liberation Front and such operational policies as taxation, terrorism and subversion. Excerpts from selected Viet Cong propaganda leaflets reveal the Front's approach to divergent groups ranging from mountain tribes to U.S. servicemen.

The concluding portion of the study treats the vital issue of foreign, i.e., Soviet and Chinese, attitudes and support. Not only are the individual policies and actions of Moscow and Peking explored through key documents and analyses, but their intense differences over the issue also emerge from the texts of their own pronouncements.

Some one hundred individual documents, a number of them direct translations, are accompanied by analytical comment which places the information in context.

II

Communist Objectives in Vietnam: the Theory and Strategy of "People's War"

Communist strategy and objectives in Vietnam are multi-faceted. In attempting to define the goals of the Communist powers in the Vietnamese struggle, one might think in terms of an Oriental "box within a box within a box." Of course, the Vietnam problem involves more than the objectives of the Communist states, which are neither monolithically fused nor mutually exclusive. There are many other diverse elements which affect Communist strategy: the lingering aftereffects of colonialism, the present Western impact, bourgeois nationalism, poverty, the urge to modernize, racial and linguistic problems, and—frequently underemphasized—the bitter passions and hatreds aroused in the Vietnamese people by 25 years of almost incessant conflict.

Nevertheless, the primary reason for conflict in South Vietnam today is Communism's attempt to gain its ends in that unfortunate country by violence. In defining the objectives of Communist strategy at its various levels, one can see that the most localized element is the Viet Cong's desire to effect the overthrow of the Saigon government and to replace it by one controlled or dominated by the National Liberation Front,

the Viet Cong's political arm. Furthermore, the North Vietnamese leaders have clearly stated many times that their goal
is the destruction of the southern republic, since it is a "lackey"
of American imperialism and stands in the way of the "legitimate" aspirations of the Vietnamese people for a unified
"fatherland" free of foreign domination. While Hanoi con-
cedes a "temporary" existence for a separate southern state after
a Viet Cong victory, it foresees a rapid sequence of steps which
would lead to a reunification of all Vietnam under President
Ho Chi Minh's control. Considering the marginal state of the
economy in North Vietnam, one can surmise that exploitation
of the agricultural resources of the South would be an immediate Hanoi objective, regardless of the timetable for reunification following a Viet Cong victory. Furthermore, North
Vietnam's activities in Laos and in the eastern border regions
of Cambodia lead to the conclusion that there probably are
larger expansionist objectives in the rest of Indochina which
Hanoi would be free to pursue once control of South Vietnam
is assured.

The story does not end in Vietnam, however. The Vietnamese Communist participants in the war may be almost
exclusively attentive to their own objectives, but as the struggle
has developed it has taken on great significance to outside
parties. Even where this importance is largely symbolic, it is an
essential part of an assessment of the roles of the other Communist powers. The war has become a substantial element in
Communist China's long-expressed desire to destroy or greatly
weaken what Peking considers the threatening American position in East Asia and it has become a major factor in China's
implicit aspiration to a dominant voice in the policies of the
Southeast Asian states. To be sure, for the indefinite future,
Peking may prefer to see the United States committed to a
costly and indecisive involvement in Vietnam.

Furthermore, the Vietnam War is not perceived by Communist China's leaders as only another vehicle for promoting the national interest in an area where Chinese influence was traditionally predominant before the coming of Western colonialism. They also have increasingly used it as a weapon in their struggle with Moscow over control of the world Communist movement and its strategy. Viewing the Vietnam conflict as the most important example of the "people's revolutionary war" it so vehemently champions, Peking apparently feels that successful conclusion of the war would be a step in pushing the international Communist movement toward a "correct line" and would greatly assist in the relegation of Soviet "revisionists" to the "dustbin" of history. Such success would also demonstrate to the other Communist parties and the emerging nations that the Maoist strategy of revolutionary violence is indeed "the great school" which will "push history forward."

Finally, for the Soviet Union, the Vietnam War represents both a dilemma and an opportunity. The extent to which the Soviets are prepared to promote and assist "national liberation" wars is uncertain. Moscow undoubtedly does not relish the prospect of the kind of total Communist victory in Vietnam which would greatly enhance China's position. At the same time, the USSR sees in this war an opportunity to capitalize on Hanoi's need for heavy armament and desire to avoid Chinese tutelage, and is therefore assisting North Vietnam materially with relatively low risk of major involvement with the United States. Furthermore, the struggle offers Moscow a chance to score points in the Sino-Soviet dispute by repeated calls for Communist unity in aiding Ho Chi Minh and the Viet Cong. Nevertheless, the Soviet view of the American position in Vietnam is ambiguous. While the USSR may have traditionally shared the Chinese and North Vietnamese desire to see American power removed entirely from that part of the world, it may be suspected that Moscow too is not entirely unhappy with the prospect of an indefinite United States commitment in Vietnam which would tie up American military power and political energies, while providing a counter to Chinese ambitions at the same time.

There have been a number of Communist-led guerrilla conflicts since World War II, and Maoist "protracted war" concepts go back 35 years. However, the Vietnam War represents the first really significant use of force against an independent nation along the lines of the newer doctrine of "people's war" or "national liberation war" as it has been more intensively developed over the last decade. The basic strategy of "people's war" is designed to challenge the West under conditions most unfavorable to it. While the Free World faced "aggression by proxy" in Korea, another element has been added in Vietnam, where the Communist pattern might be called "aggression by proxy via insurgency." Not only is this strategy calculated to get around the West's nuclear deterrent, but also, by means of internal war within the victim nation, to avoid the kind of response the United Nations made in Korea to direct aggression by a proxy state across a border. A successful insurgency cannot be developed unless it is based on some degree of genuine internal discontent, and Communist strategy entails exploitation of the indigenous elements to the fullest, in order to blur the issue of outside intervention on behalf of the rebels.

Lenin Propounds a Doctrine: Stalin Distorts It

Despite the recentness of its application in a non-colonial context, the doctrine of "national liberation wars" has long been recognized by Communist thinkers and policy-makers. Mao Tse-tung is most closely associated with the concept of "people's war," having generally been credited with synthesizing and universalizing its theory and tactical principles; however, the early Soviet leaders had recognized to some degree the potential of this kind of struggle many years before Mao's pronouncements.

Lenin developed the idea that imperialism was a higher and later form of capitalism which would somewhat delay the world's transition to socialism. He foresaw the great damage which could be inflicted on the Western imperial nations, despite their overwhelming material superiority, by prolonged popular armed struggle in the colonies. He recognized how different from Western Europe and Russia were the economic and social factors in colonial countries and realized that revolutionary tactics would have to be modified to suit varying objective circumstances. Furthermore, he acccepted the need for temporary Communist alliances with bourgeois democratic nationalists, thus foreshadowing that important element of Maoist revolutionary strategy, the United Front.

In an address on November 22, 1919, to the Second All-Russian Congress of Communist Organizations of the Peoples of the East, Lenin gave his view of the "colossal and epochal" significance to Asia and the colonial world of the Bolshevik triumph in Russia:

> It will show the peoples of the East that, weak as they may be, and invincible as may seem the power of the European oppressors, who employ in the struggle all the marvels of technology and the art of war—nevertheless, a revolutionary war waged by oppressed peoples, if it really succeeds in arousing the millions of toilers and exploited, harbours within it such potentialities, such miracles, that the emancipation of the peoples of the East is now quite practicable.
> . . .
>
> The majority of the Eastern peoples are in a worse position than the most backward country in Europe—Russia.

But in our struggle against feudal survivals and capitalism, we succeeded in uniting the peasants and workers of Russia; and our struggle proceeded so easily because the peasants and workers united against capitalism and feudalism. Here contact with the peoples of the East is particularly important, because the majority of the Eastern peoples are typical representatives of the toiling masses—not the workers who have passed through the school of the capitalist mills and factories, but typical representatives of the toiling, exploited peasant masses who are victims of mediaeval oppression. . . .

You will have to tackle these problems and solve them by your own independent experience. In that you will be assisted, on the one hand, by close alliance with the vanguard of all the toilers of other countries, and, on the other, by ability to find the right approach to the peoples of the East whom you here represent. You will have to base yourselves on that bourgeois nationalism which is awakening, and cannot but awaken, among those peoples, and which has its historical justification. At the same time, you must find your way to the toiling and exploited masses of every country and tell them in the language they understand that their only reliable hope of emancipation lies in the victory of the international revolution, and that the international proletariat is the only ally of all the hundreds of millions of toiling and exploited peoples of the East.[1]

However, Lenin realized that there was no working class in the Western sense in the colonial countries and that the immediate establishment of a dictatorship of the proletariat was not a valid concept. The relative lack of laboring class development in the predominantly peasant communities of Asia necessitated Communist cooperation—with certain reservations

---

[1] V. I. Lenin, *The National Liberation Movement in the East,* Moscow: Foreign Languages Publishing House, 1957, pp. 226, 234, 235, 236. (A collection of Lenin's commentaries on the subject.)

and safeguards—in national independence movements led by non-Communists.

On June 5, 1920, Lenin presented to the Second Congress of the Communist International his "Preliminary Draft of Theses on the National and Colonial Questions." This statement carried forward the idea of Soviet alliance with "national liberation" movements and presented a rationale for cooperation with bourgeois democratic elements:

> From these fundamental premises it follows that the whole policy of the Communist International on the national and colonial questions should rest on closer union of the proletarians and working masses generally of all nations and countries for a joint revolutionary struggle to overthrow the landlords and the bourgeoisie. For this alone will guarantee victory over capitalism, without which the abolition of national oppression and inequality is impossible. . . .
>
> . . . One cannot confine oneself at the present time to the bare recognition or proclamation of the need for closer union between the working people of the various nations; it is necessary to pursue a policy that will achieve the closest alliance of all the national and colonial liberation movements with Soviet Russia, the form of this alliance to be determined by the degree of development of the communist movement among the proletariat of each country, or of the bourgeois-democratic liberation movement of the workers and peasants in backward countries or among backward nationalities. . . .
>
> . . . The Communist International must enter into a temporary alliance with bourgeois democracy in colonial and backward countries, but must not merge with it and must under all circumstances uphold the independence of the proletarian movement even if in its most embryonic form. . . .[2]

---

[2] *Ibid.*, pp. 251, 252, 255.

As the years went by, the USSR gave its support in varying degree to anti-Western movements in the colonial world, but with the national interests of the Soviet Union always taking precedence over the fate of any particular revolutionary party or movement. In the Stalin period Moscow never developed any serious programs for broadly-conceived movements based on the peasant masses, preferring instead to work through labor leaders, educated revolutionaries, and clandestine agents— nearly always expecting far too much from ill-conceived and poorly-organized urban uprisings, general strikes, and terror campaigns. Stalin's clumsy China adventure of the 1920's was an example of Soviet failure to come to grips with the realities of Asian life and political dynamics. Mao Tse-tung therefore became, almost by default, the predominant figure in the development of the theory and practice of protracted "people's war" based on the Asian peasant masses. Moscow was involved in a number of uprisings, beginning in 1948, which created serious situations of varying duration in India, Burma, Malaya and Indonesia, but on the whole, direct Soviet participation in the epochal process which brought an end to the Western imperial system in Asia after World War II was quite small.

Khrushchev Revives Soviet Interest in "Liberation Wars"

After the death of Stalin, however, Moscow began to play a more active political and economic role in the emerging world of Asia and Africa. Although the USSR generally accepted the bourgeois-nationalist leadership of the newly independent states, it began to look with increasing favor, at least in a theoretical way, on the concept of "national liberation war" in certain areas of Asia, Africa, and Latin America as a potentially useful device during an era of mutual nuclear deterrence in which even limited conventional engagement with Western forces would be fraught with extreme hazard.

Khrushchev propounded the basic modern Soviet view of "national liberation wars" in his famous January 1961 report on the earlier meeting of the 81 world Communist parties in Moscow:

> Now about *national liberation* wars. The armed struggle of the Vietnamese people or the war of the Algerian people, now in its seventh year, is a recent example of such a war.
>
> These wars began as uprisings of colonial peoples against their oppressors, developing into guerrilla wars.
>
> There will be wars of liberation as long as imperialism exists, as long as colonialism exists. These are revolutionary wars. Such wars are not only possible but inevitable, since the colonialists will not voluntarily grant the peoples independence. Therefore the people can win their freedom and independence only through struggle, including armed struggle. . . .
>
> Can such wars occur in the future? They can. Can there be such uprisings? There can. These are precisely wars of popular rebellion. Can conditions in other countries come to a point where the people exhaust their patience and rise up with arms in hand? They can. What attitude do Marxists have toward such uprisings? The most favorable. These uprisings must not be identified with wars among states, with local wars, because in these uprisings the people are fighting to exercise their right to self-determination and for their social and independent national development; these are uprisings against rotten reactionary regimes and against colonialists. Communists fully and unreservedly support such just wars and march in the van of the peoples fighting wars of liberation.[3]

---

[3] *Pravda,* January 25, 1961.

One would imagine that such a ringing declaration in a major document of the world Communist movement would bring forth rapid development of specific Soviet doctrine on "national liberation wars"—how they should be fought and the extent of Soviet assistance to such "just" struggles. Actually this has not been the case. The relatively small amount of commentary on this subject produced by Soviet military and political writers has in fact resulted in some doctrinal confusion.

Soviet thinking rejects local limited conventional war as too dangerous; however, the logical extension of a Soviet pledge of assistance to "liberation forces" might be the initiation of local U.S.-Soviet conventional conflict expanding eventually into general war. Soviet statements have been purposely vague on the crucial question of whether the concrete support the USSR is prepared to render will include Soviet forces in military situations arising from a "national liberation war." [4] Soviet pronouncements have recently grown somewhat stronger, and Moscow has become increasingly involved in Vietnam, both because of the opportunities presented and the issue of the Chinese competitive challenge. Nevertheless, no real body of doctrine has emerged, and ambiguity on certain key issues of Soviet support remains the order of the day.

Mao Produces a General Theory of "People's War"

The spotty character of Soviet response to the national independence drive and to the peasant-based revolutionary movements in East Asia has left the field of strategy formulation

---

[4] Thomas W. Wolfe, *Soviet Strategy at the Crossroads,* Cambridge: Harvard University Press, 1964, pp. 124-127. See also V. D. Sokolovsky, *Soviet Military Strategy* (RAND Corp. Translation), Englewood Cliffs: Prentice Hall, 1963.

largely to Mao and his colleagues. The published works of Mao are considered to have universalized the experiences of the Chinese Communists and to have produced a general theory of "revolutionary people's war," while at the same time recognizing the importance of differences in the political, economic, and social situations in various countries.

Mao's laurels as an architect of revolutionary doctrine would have been less meaningful had it not been for two great events which gave his strategy the undeniable aura of success: the victory of the Communist revolution in China, followed by the destruction of French colonial rule in Vietnam at the hands of the Communist-led Viet Minh independence movement which drew much of its inspiration from the Chinese example. What makes the Maoist doctrine of "people's war" so important to Vietnam today is that in this one area of East Asia the movement which ejected the European colonial power was based largely on those principles of protracted struggle enunciated by the Chinese oracle. Furthermore, the present armed campaign of the National Liberation Front of South Vietnam (NLF) to complete the Communist conquest of the country draws its basic inspiration from the same source.

Regardless of the earlier hopes the Viet Cong may have had for attaining power through a Bolshevik-style uprising in the urban areas of South Vietnam and among the armed forces of the Saigon government,[5] the fundamental doctrinal and operational patterns of Viet Cong insurgency find their roots in the Chinese and Viet Minh revolutionary experience. The Viet Cong are ardent disciples of Mao and the revolutionary theories expressed in his many written works. They also utilize the

---

[5] Douglas Pike, "How Strong Is the NLF?" in *The Reporter*, February 24, 1966, p. 23. This aspect of NLF strategy is more fully explored in Pike's excellent larger work, *Viet Cong*, Cambridge: M.I.T. Press, 1966.

related principles laid down by General Vo Nguyen Giap, the Viet Minh general who led the fight against the French on "people's war" principles.

While armed force as the ultimate arbiter of conflict is an essential part of Leninist political theory, Mao Tse-tung's revolutionary thought is especially permeated by military usage. His relish for armed combat, drawn largely from his rather romantic view of the military heroes of China's past, is illustrated over and over again in the military figures of speech he applies to the solution of many kinds of problems.[6] Essentially, Mao brushes aside the sophistries with which some Western observers have attempted to explain the dynamics of the Chinese Communist revolution and comes directly to the point. For instance, he discusses with fierce clarity some aspects of the use of military force in *Problems of War and Strategy*, written in November 1938:

> The seizure of power by armed force, the settlement of the issue by war, is the central task and the highest form of revolution. This Marxist-Leninist principle of revolution holds good universally, for China and for all other countries. . . .
>
> Every Communist must grasp the truth, "political power grows out of the barrel of a gun." Our principle is that the Party commands the gun, and the gun must never be allowed to command the Party. Yet, having guns, we can create Party organizations. . . . We can also create cadres, create schools, create culture, create mass movements. . . . All things grow out of the barrel of a gun. According to the Marxist theory of the state, the army is the chief component of state power. Whoever wants to seize and retain state power must have a strong army. Some people ridicule

---

[6] See a study of this aspect of Maoist thought in Stuart R. Schram, "The 'Military Deviation' of Mao Tse-tung" in *Problems of Communism*, January-February 1964, pp. 49-56.

us as advocates of the "omnipotence of war." Yes, we are advocates of the omnipotence of revolutionary war; that is good, not bad, it is Marxist. . . . Experience in the class struggle in the era of imperialism teaches us that it is only by the power of the gun that the working class and the labouring masses can defeat the armed bourgeoisie and landlords; in this sense we may say that only with guns can the whole world be transformed. We are advocates of the abolition of war, we do not want war; but war can only be abolished through war, and in order to get rid of the gun it is necessary to take up the gun.[7]

Mao also constructed a military model for revolutionary war in his essay *On Protracted War* in May 1938. This basic structural formulation has subsequently been widely discussed by Communist and Western military thinkers:

Since the Sino-Japanese war is a protracted one and final victory will belong to China, it can reasonably be assumed that this protracted war will pass through three stages. The first stage covers the period of the enemy's strategic offensive and our strategic defensive. The second stage will be the period of the enemy's strategic consolidation and our preparation for the counter-offensive. The third stage will be the period of our strategic counter-offensive and the enemy's strategic retreat.[8]

At the same time, Mao never lost sight of the political purposes which give direction to armed struggle. In fact, he constantly emphasized the primacy of politics, particularly in exploiting the weaknesses of his opponent. He clearly recognized the need for political and social mobilization of the normally apathetic masses and appreciated the advantages of astute propaganda, a moderate-sounding political program, exploita-

---

[7] Mao Tse-tung, *Selected Military Writings,* Peking: Foreign Languages Press, 1963, pp. 272, 273.

[8] *Ibid.,* pp. 210, 211.

tion of nationalistic sentiment, and negotiations in a favorable climate. In preserving the primacy of politics, a strong Communist Party would always prevail over the other organs of power. Mao saw the alternating armed and peaceful (political) forces of struggle as an integrated course of revolutionary action.[9] Political aspects of revolutionary war were given primary consideration in this passage from *On Protracted War:*

> A national revolutionary war . . . cannot be won without universal and thoroughgoing political mobilization. . . . This move is crucial; it is indeed of primary importance, while our inferiority in weapons and other things is only secondary. The mobilization of the common people throughout the country will create a vast sea in which to drown the enemy, create the conditions that will make up for our inferiority in arms and other things, and create the prerequisites for overcoming every difficulty in the war. To win victory, we must persevere in the War of Resistance, in the united front and in the protracted war. But all these are inseparable from the mobilization of the common people. To wish for victory and yet neglect political mobilization is like wishing to "go north by driving a chariot south," and the result would inevitably be to forfeit victory.[10]

On Coalition Government, in April 1945, carried forward Mao's political thesis, particularly the importance of developing functional organizations which would engage every able-bodied person in endless activity under close Party scrutiny:

> Under the leadership of their democratic governments, all the . . . people are called upon to join organizations of workers, peasants, youth and women, and cultural, professional and other organizations, which will whole-

---

[9] An excellent study of these points can be found in Tang Tsou and Morton H. Halperin, "Maoism at Home and Abroad," in *Problems of Communism,* July-August 1965, pp. 1-13.

[10] Mao Tse-tung, *op. cit.,* p. 228.

heartedly perform various tasks in support of the armed forces. These tasks are not limited to rallying the people to join the army, transporting grain for the army, giving preferential treatment to soldiers' families and helping the troops in meeting their material needs. They also include mobilizing the guerrilla units, militia and self-defense corps to make widespread raids and lay land mines against the enemy, gather intelligence about the enemy, comb out traitors and spies, transport and protect the wounded and take direct part in the army's operations. At the same time, the people in all the Liberated Areas are enthusiastically taking up various kinds of political, economic, cultural and health work. The most important thing in this connection is to mobilize everybody for the production of grain and articles of daily use and to ensure that all government institutions and schools . . . devote their free time to production for their own support in order to supplement the people's and the army's production campaigns for self-sufficiency, and thus help to create a great upsurge of production for sustaining the protracted War of Resistance . . . Such is a real people's war. Only by waging such a people's war can we defeat the national enemy. . . .[11]

The Viet Minh and "People's War"

Although the Vietnamese Communists have historically been closer to the USSR, particularly in organizational matters, the Communist-led Viet Minh movement, which carried on the successful national independence war against the French from 1946 to 1954, drew much of its basic inspiration from Chinese Communist revolutionary experience. This was particularly so in the latter half of the anti-French struggle, after Mao's victorious armies arrived at the Indochina border and began to supply the Viet Minh guerrillas with the training and materiel

---

[11] *Ibid.*, p. 302.

to develop into a more or less regular light infantry army which could carry on successful conventional battle with the French Expeditionary Corps. The outstanding Viet Minh military leader of the period was General Vo Nguyen Giap, who is now North Vietnam's Defense Minister and a member of the Politburo of the Communist *Lao Dong* Party. In his classic book, *People's War, People's Army*, General Giap sums up the history and lessons of the war against the French and highlights some facets of organization for that struggle. While he does not specifically acknowledge his debt to Mao's writings on guerrilla warfare (this might imply a subordination to the Chinese which in fact did not exist), his work formulates within an acceptable Vietnamese context the essentials of Maoist revolutionary strategy. The significance of Giap's model to Communist goals in South Vietnam and elsewhere is sufficiently obvious that an American edition of his book has been subtitled "The Viet Cong Insurrection Manual for Underdeveloped Countries." Giap's summation generalized the politico-military lessons of the Indochina war and portended the bloody "reunification" struggle now following its tragic course in South Vietnam:

> Looking back, on the whole, our Party stuck to the national democratic revolutionary line throughout the Resistance War. Thanks to this, we succeeded in mobilizing our people to launch the people's war, using the enormous strength of the people to vanquish the aggressors. . . . while in foreign policy, efforts had to be made to win over the support of progressive people throughout the world, particularly to closely coordinate with the struggle of the French people . . . against this dirty war. . . .

> The enemy's . . . weak point lay in the unjust character of his war. As a result, he was internally divided, not supported by the people of his own country and did not enjoy the sympathy of world opinion. . . . Our strong

point lay in the just nature of our Resistance War. Hence, we succeeded in uniting our entire people. . . .

. . . In general, our Resistance War was a guerrilla war moving gradually to regular war, from guerrilla warfare to mobile warfare combined with partial entrenched camp warfare . . . Guerrilla warfare is the form of fighting of the masses of the people, of the people of a weak and badly equipped country, who stand up against an aggressive army which possesses better equipment and technique. This is the way of fighting the revolutionary war which relies on the heroic spirit to triumph over modern weapons, avoiding the enemy when he is the stronger and attacking him when he is the weaker, now scattering, now regrouping one's own forces, now wearing out, now exterminating the enemy, determined to fight him everywhere, so that wherever the enemy goes he would be submerged in a sea of armed people who hit back at him, thus undermining his spirit and exhausting his forces. . . .

. . . To keep itself in life and develop, guerrilla warfare has necessarily to develop into mobile warfare. This is a general law. . . . If guerrilla warfare did not move to mobile warfare, not only the strategic task of annihilating the enemy manpower could not be carried out, but even guerrilla activities could not be maintained and extended. . . .

These were the strategy and tactics of the people's war, the art of military conduct of the people's war, of the revolutionary war in a small and backward agricultural country under the leadership of our Party. . . .

At present, North Vietnam is entirely liberated; it is the vast rear of our army . . . Proceeding from the revolutionary task in the present stage, our rear is, on a national scale, the entirely liberated North Vietnam which is advancing to socialism. *It is the revolutionary base for the whole country. . . .*[12]

---

[12] Vo Nguyen Giap, *People's War, People's Army* (Amer. ed.), New York: Frederick A. Praeger, 1962, pp. 96-146. Italics added.

Giap's guerrilla and light infantry forces fought a war of independence against a hated colonial occupier. The Communist forces today are carrying on what they consider to be a continuation of the struggle to "liberate" Vietnam. Their opponents do not accept this continuity of purpose, but rather see Communist strategy as an attempt to use the anti-imperialist theme as a rationale for aggression. To be sure, it is not the traditional kind of aggression. Both native and imported guerrillas are used in a way which makes it very difficult to define the present action as an aggression in terms of international law. The complexities and obscurity inherent in such an insurgency are part of the strategy. However, the kind of war the Communists fight in South Vietnam does create other problems for its leaders. For instance, Giap does not provide in his model for overcoming difficulties in mobilizing popular support when there is no immediately recognizable colonial enemy, but the massive propaganda campaigns and continuous coercive measures carried out daily by the Viet Cong in the South Vietnamese countryside speak for themselves on this point.[13]

Lin Piao Restates the Theory and Practice of Revolutionary War

On September 3, 1965, the 20th anniversary of the victory over Japan, there appeared a most significant article by Lin Piao, Communist China's Defense Minister and possible heir to Mao's mantle. Entitled "Long Live the Victory of People's War!," this lengthy work is a basic recapitulation of the theory and practice of revolutionary war as seen by the Chinese Communists. It is probably the strongest and most unequivocal

---

[13] An excellent commentary on the significance of Giap's book may be found in Roger Hilsman's foreword to the Praeger edition previously cited.

statement to emerge in some years on the basic doctrinal and operational requirements of the type of revolutionary violence espoused by Peking. While it sets no essentially new courses, it pulls together in a most militant manner much that has been said by Mao and others in piecemeal fashion over the years, and as such it ranks as a major document of Chinese Communism.

As a whole or in part, Marshal Lin's article is open to varying interpretations, not necessarily mutually exclusive. It certainly is an attempt to formulate a systematic application of Maoist revolutionary war doctrine to the present world situation and to the future requirements of revolutionary movements in the emerging nations. In striving to discredit the Soviet Union's view of "national liberation wars," Lin castigates it as timid and passive, desiring only the localization of such conflicts for fear of escalation to nuclear war. There is also a full-scale attack on the United States and all other governments interested in world progress through peace and stability. What is most difficult to judge is what Lin is trying to say in regard to Communist China's future world policy. The article may not be a blueprint for charting this course, since the realities of the international power configuration will undoubtedly frustrate Peking in the pursuit of optimum goals, but it does clearly express the probable direction of Chinese encouragement and support when favorable revolutionary opportunities arise.

Our main concern at this point is with Lin's attempt to apply Mao's revolutionary model to the underdeveloped areas of the world classified as "storm centers of revolution" and his bid for Chinese Communist leadership of such revolutions. Some of the flavor of this aspect of the article can be gathered from the following excerpts:

> . . . Comrade Mao Tse-tung's great merit lies in the fact that he has succeeded in integrating the universal truth of

Marxism-Leninism with the concrete practice of the Chinese revolution and has enriched and developed Marxism-Leninism by his masterly generalization and summation of the experience gained during the Chinese people's protracted revolutionary struggle. . . .

Comrade Mao Tse-tung's theory of people's war has been proved by the long practice of the Chinese revolution to be in accord with the objective laws of such wars and to be invincible. It has not only been valid for China, it is a great contribution to the revolutionary struggles of the oppressed nations and peoples throughout the world. . . .

The history of people's war in China and other countries provides conclusive evidence that the growth of the people's revolutionary forces from weak and small beginnings into strong and large forces is a universal law of development of people's war. A people's war inevitably meets with many difficulties, with ups and downs and setbacks in the course of its development, but no force can alter its general trend toward inevitable triumph. . . .

It must be emphasized that Comrade Mao Tse-tung's theory of the establishment of rural revolutionary base areas and the encirclement of the cities from the countryside is of outstanding and universal practical importance for the present revolutionary struggles of all the oppressed nations and peoples.

. . . Taking the entire globe, if North America and Western Europe can be called "the cities of the world," then Asia, Africa, and Latin America constitute "the rural areas of the world." In a sense, the contemporary world revolution also presents a picture of the encirclement of cities by the rural areas. In the final analysis, the whole cause of world revolution hinges on the revolutionary struggles of the Asian, African, and Latin American peoples who make up the overwhelming majority of the world's population. . . .

Since World War II, U.S. imperialism has stepped into
the shoes of German, Japanese and Italian fascism and has
been trying to build a great American empire by dominat-
ing and enslaving the whole world. It is the most rabid
aggressor in human history and the most ferocious common enemy of the people of the world. Every people or
country in the world that wants revolution, independence
and peace cannot but direct the spearhead of its struggle
against U.S. imperialism. . . .

At present, the main battlefield of the fierce struggle
between the people of the world on the one side and U.S.
imperialism and its lackeys on the other is the vast area of
Asia, Africa and Latin America. Since World War II, revolutionary storms have been rising in this area, and today
they have become the most important force directly pound-
ing U.S. imperialism. . . .

Vietnam is the most convincing current example of a
victim of aggression defeating U.S. imperialism by a people's war. The United States has made South Vietnam a
testing ground for the suppression of people's war. It has
carried on this experiment for many years, and everybody
can now see that the U.S. aggressors are unable to find a
way of coping with people's war.

History has proved and will go on proving that people's
war is the most effective weapon against U.S. imperialism
and its lackeys. U.S. imperialism, like a mad bull dashing
from place to place, will finally be burned to ashes in the
blazing fire of the people's wars it has provoked by its own
actions.[14]

It is clear from some of Lin's statements that the Chinese
Communists count on a revolutionary tide in the "third world"
to neutralize the present international power balance which
weighs heavily against China and prevents the realization of
Peking's external goals. There is a hope, however unrealistic,

---

[14] *Peking Review*, No. 36, September 3, 1965.

that this tide might help Communist China achieve the removal of American influence from East Asia, the recovery of Taiwan, and the breakup of what Peking sees as an American-Soviet monopoly of world power. Implicit is the expectation that the military strength of the United States will be seriously diffused and weakened in coping with revolutionary wars around the world. This is especially evident in the graphic forecast of the encirclement and strangulation of the "world cities" of Europe and North America by the underdeveloped "rural" areas of the globe in Asia, Africa and Latin America.

Some observers see in the Lin document a large measure of advice and admonition to Hanoi and the Viet Cong. It does appear to say that the Communists in Vietnam should concentrate on fighting the war as a national war of resistance against the United States in the manner of the anti-Japanese war in China, and should play down some of the more extreme elements of civil conflict within South Vietnam. In stressing repeatedly that each revolutionary people must rely on its own resources in carrying on its struggle, Lin implies strongly that China has no intention of entering the fray with its military forces, but will continue support of Hanoi and the Viet Cong short of this. This, of course, may be subject to change.

Furthermore, in passages playing up the exemplary conduct of Chinese Communist forces in both the anti-Japanese and civil wars, there are some definite hints that Peking may be unhappy with certain excesses in Viet Cong operational methods which could prove counterproductive, e.g., large-scale terrorism. At the same time, by proclaiming "inevitable" victory for "people's war," the article provides a "pep talk," perhaps to bolster Viet Cong morale during a period of military reverses. In short, Lin has provided a manual of instruction on how and how not to fight a successful revolutionary struggle.

One virtue required for success is self-reliance. "People's war" as a "do it yourself" operation is illustrated in Lin's article in this manner:

> The peoples of the world invariably support each other in their struggles against imperialism and its lackeys. Those countries which have won victory are duty-bound to support and aid the peoples who have not yet done so. Nevertheless, foreign aid can only play a supplementary role.
>
> In order to make a revolution and to fight a people's war and be victorious, it is imperative to adhere to the policy of self-reliance, rely on the strength of the masses in one's own country and prepare to carry on the fight independently even when all material aid from outside is cut off. If one does not operate by one's own efforts, does not independently ponder and solve the problems of the revolution in one's country and does not rely on the strength of the masses, but leans wholly on foreign aid—even though this be aid from socialist countries which persist in revolution—no victory can be won, or be consolidated even if it is won.[15]

With these words, Lin is making it plain that there is a clear limit to the aid China will give insurgent movements. Nowhere does Lin seem to indicate that China's "firm support and aid" to foreign revolutionary struggles will go so far as to risk a major direct clash with the United States.

---

[15] *Ibid.*

III

Hanoi's War: a Violent Road to "Peaceful Reunification"

The Geneva Accords of 1954 which partitioned Vietnam reflected the actual military situation of the time more accurately than would be admitted by those who claim the Viet Minh had really won the right to control the entire country. Nonetheless, there were elements in Ho Chi Minh's entourage who felt that pressure from the Soviet Union to accept the partition at Geneva had cheated the Viet Minh out of the full fruits of victory over France. However, the Communists may have calculated that the nationwide "free" elections called for by 1956 in the political declaration attached to the Geneva armistice would surely result in the consummation of their control. Although they may have entertained doubts that the elections would actually be held, they knew the Viet Minh were the only organized and cohesive political force of any consequence in Vietnam, and since the southern half was ravaged by war and politically fragmented, a confident expectation that the South would somehow fall under Hanoi's control seemed amply justified in the early post-Geneva period. Although the flight of nearly a million people from North to South after Geneva was a great moral and psychological victory for the Diem government, the immense resettlement problems arising from this influx added to the almost unbelievable burdens of the southern regime in trying to cope with chaos.

Hanoi's Commitment to the Destruction of the Southern Republic

For the first few years after Geneva, Hanoi was generally content to avoid violence and to push the southern revolution on the political level, while concentrating its efforts on the consolidation of the *Lao Dong's* control at home in North Vietnam, on the rebuilding and expansion of the northern economy and army, and on coping with the serious problems surrounding the harsh "land reform" program in the North. The cadres and sympathizers in the South could spend the time usefully preparing an organization which would be ready to take over when the "rotten" Diem regime fell or unification elections were held. Political penetration of the southern villages and the subversion of disaffected non-Communist leadership in South Vietnam were the order of the day. Furthermore, the USSR apparently discouraged an early resumption of hostilities by Hanoi.

President Diem's survival against heavy odds, the steady increase of his power and authority, and the modest success of some of his programs combined to kill one element of North Vietnam's expectations. Hanoi's hopes were further dashed by Diem's refusal to agree to the 1956 elections and by the election that year of a southern Constituent Assembly which formulated a constitution that seemed to signify the permanence of the Saigon regime. Diem's abrupt ejection of the French military and civilian advisers, on whose influence Ho Chi Minh may have relied, was a further blow. All of these factors contributed to Hanoi's decision to use force to destroy its southern neighbor.

Today's war in South Vietnam arose essentially out of Communist North Vietnam's frustration over the refusal of the southern republic to die—either through internal collapse, subversion, or Communist-dominated all-Vietnam elections. The struggle's violent phase began in the 1958-1959 period, when Hanoi found the steadily increasing stability and prosperity of South Vietnam intolerable and made its decision to eradicate its neighbor by force of arms. This commitment to the destruction by violence of the Republic of Vietnam and to the reunification of the country under Communist control has been basic to Hanoi's plan from that time.

North Vietnam's Role in the War: Both Overt and Clandestine

Hanoi has attempted to camouflage its actions by utilizing Southerners wherever possible. The Viet Cong movement has been built around two elements: first, the southern Communist Viet Minh cadres who were ordered underground after the 1954 Geneva Agreement for the purpose of political preparation, and who were reorganized and called to armed action four to five years later; and second, those significant numbers of Communist-oriented troops who elected to move to the North after the fighting against the French ended, who were retrained by the Hanoi regime for the purpose of attacking the Republic of Vietnam and who were later infiltrated into the South. Some knowledgeable observers have estimated that 3,000 to 5,000 southern Communist military and political cadres were left behind after the 1954 Accords. The heaviest concentrations were in the areas where Viet Minh strength had been greatest during the anti-French war: four provinces on the central coast, the "Red" zone north of Saigon, the Plain of Reeds near the Cambodian border, two Mekong Delta provinces, and the southernmost Ca Mau Peninsula. These were the cadres who prepared the ground for the shooting war. Their cached armament, while mostly old weapons from the 1946-54 war, was not inconsiderable. In the years before 1959 the Saigon authorities reported to the International Control Commission (provided for in the Geneva Armistice to supervise the execution of the Accords, but with no enforcement powers) that hundreds of hidden arms and ammunition dumps had been discovered by Diem's army and police.

In 1959 there began a large-scale movement of personnel from the North into South Vietnam—not a traditional invasion, but an infiltration homeward of Southerners who had gone North in 1954 and had been retrained. They came by sea or via the Ho Chi Minh Trail in Laos. They returned to their native areas to participate in the shooting war which had just begun, and by operating within the protective circle of family and friends they gave a useful Southern coloration to the enterprise. Hanoi's attempts to preserve appearances gradually began to lose their effectiveness, however, and as the scale of insurgent attacks against the Saigon government rose over the years, Northern troops and political cadres were used in increasing numbers to bolster the Viet Cong. Similarly, as combat requirements soared, the proportion of North Vietnamese weapons and supplies in the rebel inventory greatly increased.

Hanoi's political organization for the war has developed steadily. As early as 1955, the North Vietnamese established a Fatherland Front to make propaganda from Hanoi on the subject of reunification. While it has worked energetically at this task ever since, there is no real evidence that it has accomplished much, as reunification has never become a burning issue. Therefore, Hanoi's major attention in the early years was concentrated on the building of the local infrastructure in the South designed to influence and then control the peasant population—the village cells and committees, the various mass functional organizations, the progaganda teams, and the embryonic military units, as well as a network of political cadres, administrative personnel, couriers, special agents and so on.

As Diem's rule increasingly alienated segments of the South Vietnamese elite, a few of them began to assist the Viet Cong cause. In order to capture as broad a spectrum of Southern support as possible, or at least to give the impression that wide Southern allegiance to its revolution existed, Hanoi considered in 1960 that the time was ripe for a more formal overt political organization to direct the war within the South. At the Third Congress of the *Lao Dong* Party, held in Hanoi in September 1960, a number of resolutions and speeches important to the war in the South were forthcoming. Among them were very emphatic statements on the dominant role the North would play in the struggle and a call for a "united front" organization. Guidelines were established for what was to become the National Front for the Liberation of South Vietnam (the NLF).

The resolution of the Third National Congress of the *Lao Dong* Party adopted at Hanoi on September 10, 1960, included the following analysis and directive:

> The People's democratic power, more and more consolidated, is a strong instrument for fulfilling the tasks of proletarian dictatorship and speeding up socialist transformation and socialist construction in the North; at the same time, it is a firm base for our whole people in their struggle for the strengthening of peace and the achievement of national reunification. . . .

> In the present state, the Vietnamese revolution has two strategic tasks: first, to carry out the socialist revolution in North Vietnam; second, to liberate South Vietnam from the ruling yoke of the U.S. imperialists and their henchmen in order to achieve national unity and complete independence and freedom throughout the country. These two

strategic tasks are closely related to each other and spur each other forward. . . . in the South we must endeavor to rally all national and democratic forces, expand and consolidate the national unity bloc, isolate the U.S. imperialists and their henchmen, and speed up the struggle to strengthen peace and reunify our Fatherland. . . .

To insure the complete success of the revolutionary struggle in South Vietnam, our people there must strive to establish a united bloc of workers, peasants, and soldiers and to bring into being a broad national united front directed against the U.S.-Diem clique and based on the worker-peasant alliance. This front must rally all the patriotic classes and sections of the people, the majority and minority nationalities, all patriotic parties and religious groupings, together with all individuals inclined to oppose the U.S.-Diem clique. . . .

The front must carry out its work in a very flexible manner in order to rally all forces that can be rallied, win over all forces that can be won over, neutralize all forces that should be neutralized, and draw the broad masses into the general struggle against the U.S.-Diem clique for the liberation of the South and the peaceful reunification of the Fatherland.

The revolutionary movement in the South plays a very important role in relation to the reunification of the country. Simultaneously with the effort to build the North and advance toward socialism our people must strive to maintain and develop the revolutionary forces in the South and create favorable conditions for peaceful national reunification. . . .[16]

President Ho Chi Minh has always expressed his regime's goals rather succinctly. From his speech at the opening session

---

[16] Department of State, *A Threat to the Peace, Part II,* Washington, D.C.: Government Printing Office, 1961, pp. 1, 2.

of the *Lao Dong* Party's Third Congress in Hanoi, September 5, 1960:

> A prosperous and strong North is the firm base of the struggle for national reunification. This congress will shed new light on our people's revolutionary path to peaceful national reunification. Our nation is one, our country is one. Our people will undoubtedly overcome all difficulties, achieve national reunification and bring the North and South together again. . . .[17]

In a typical demonstration of Communist semantics, Defense Minister Vo Nguyen Giap put the war in a "peace" context as he laid out the following to the Third Congress on September 12:

> After thoroughly surveying the international and domestic situation, the political report of the party Central Committee sets forth the revolutionary task to be carried out by our people in the present phase as follows: to strengthen the unity of all the people; to struggle resolutely to maintain peace; to accelerate the socialist revolution in North Vietnam while at the same time stepping up the national people's democratic revolution in South Vietnam; to achieve national reunification on the basis of independence and democracy, to build a peaceful, unified, independent, democratic, rich, and strong Vietnam, and to contribute practically to reinforcing the socialist camp and to maintaining peace in Southeast Asia and in the world. . . .[18]

In April 1961, one of the most militant members of the Hanoi inner circle, Truong Chinh, expressed a much franker view of the "peaceful" way in which the South was to be "liberated." Writing for the benefit of the Party elite and cadres in the Hanoi political and theoretical monthly *Hoc Tap,*

---

[17] *Ibid.,* p. 3.

[18] *Ibid.,* p. 4.

he drew a clear blueprint for Communist takeover of the whole country:

> However, we are firmly convinced that the revolution in South Vietnam and the struggle to achieve peaceful national reunification will surely succeed because they are evolving under these favorable conditions: socialist North Vietnam is being rapidly consolidated and strengthened, is providing good support to the South Vietnamese revolution, and is serving as a strong basis for the struggle for national reunification . . .

> Unable to endure the oppressive, exploiting, and murderous policies of the enemy, southern compatriots have to rise and group themselves under the fighting banner of the Liberation Front to destroy the U.S.-Diem regime and set up a national democratic coalition government. Once established, this government will agree with the DRV Government about achieving peaceful national reunification under one form or another, including the holding of free elections throughout the country. Thus, though South Vietnam will be liberated by nonpeaceful means, the Party policy of achieving peaceful national reunification is still correct. . . .[19]

While most observers give Hanoi credit for basic inspiration and strong logistic support in the Vietnam guerrilla war, the crux of the issue over defining the struggle as a real aggression or as a genuine South Vietnamese civil war and social revolution lies in the existence and degree of North Vietnam's leadership and operational control of the Viet Cong movement. Any assertion that such leadership and control do not exist is difficult to reconcile with the available facts. Although the evidence of *total* Hanoi control of the Viet Cong may not be complete, it does constitute the bulk of the data. The direction, control, and support of the Communist effort in the South by the Party,

---

[19] *Ibid.*, pp. 6, 7.

governmental and military apparatus in North Vietnam have been demonstrated and documented. Neither NLF nor Hanoi spokesmen and media are reticent about admitting the leadership of the enterprise by the *Lao Dong* and Ho Chi Minh; they seem to be more evasive only about the infiltration of Northern manpower, despite the numerous Communist prisoners and defectors who have confirmed the presence of organized units of the People's Army of North Vietnam, and who in some cases have described the control apparatus manned by Northern cadres.

Furthermore, there is no demonstrable evidence of *significant* differences in the output of NLF and Hanoi propaganda organs, despite periodic hints from various outside quarters that important conflicts between the two are about to appear. Most successful revolutionary undertakings do generate a certain independent momentum, and there may well be non-Communist Southerners in the Liberation Front who wish more freedom from Hanoi's grip, but a claim that these men do have such freedom slides over several hard facts: the intricate interlocking cell structure of control in Communist-dominated movements, the lack of any strong independent political base by non-Communist NLF leaders, and the absence of any significant information attesting to autonomy or freedom of maneuver.

Hanoi's direction of both the political and military aspects of the guerrilla war is very clearly laid out in the U.S. State Department's White Papers of 1961 and 1965, the information in both presumably having been distilled from intelligence collection and analysis over a considerable period of time. Although the 1965 document has been attacked as a hastily-conceived and distorted apology for the American decision to intervene in the Vietnam fighting, it was based to a considerable degree on evidence produced in the generally well-received earlier White Paper, and its basic exposition of Communist strategy, tactics and organization in South Vietnam has not been successfully impeached. The following excerpt summarizes the organizational framework of North Vietnamese domination of the Viet Cong movement:

> The VC military and political apparatus in South Vietnam is an extension of an elaborate military and political structure in North Vietnam which directs and supplies it with the tools for conquest. . . .
>
> Political direction and control of the Viet Cong is supplied by the *Lao Dong* Party, i.e. the Communist Party, led by Ho Chi Minh. . . .
>
> Overall direction of the VC movement is the responsibility of the Central Committee of the *Lao Dong* Party. Within the Central Committee a special Reunification Department has been established. . . . It lays down broad strategy for the movement to conquer South Vietnam.
>
> . . . The Central Committee, through its Reunification Department, issues directives to the Central Office [for South Vietnam], which translates them into specific orders for the appropriate subordinate command.
>
> Under the Central Office are six regional units. . . . A regional committee responsible to the Central Office directs VC activities in each region. . . .
>
> Below each regional committee are similarly structured units at the province and district levels. At the base of the Communist pyramid are the individual party cells, which may be organized on a geographic base or within social or occupational groups. . . .
>
> The National Front for the Liberation of South Vietnam is the screen behind which the Communists carry out their program of conquest. It is the creature of the Communist Government in Hanoi. . . . It was designed to create the illusion that the Viet Cong campaign of subversion was truly indigenous to South Vietnam rather than an externally directed Communist plan. . . .

Military affairs of the Viet Cong are the responsibility of the High Command of the People's Army of North Vietnam and the Ministry of Defense, under close supervision from the *Lao Dong* Party. . . .

The military structure of the Viet Cong is an integral part of the political machinery that controls every facet of VC activity in South Vietnam under Hanoi's overall direction. . . .[20]

After the establishment of the Liberation Front, Hanoi reorganized the Southern arm of the Communist (*Lao Dong*) Party as the "vanguard" element of the movement and gave it a new name which would lend it the appearance of being only an indigenous Marxist component of a union of diverse "patriotic" groups. This move was designed to explain Communist presence in the Front, but to disguise Marxist control of it. In fact, however, the true nature of this People's Revolutionary Party was revealed in a Viet Cong document captured in May 1962 in Ba Xuyen province which contained instructions from the provincial committee of the *Lao Dong* Party to the district committees in the provinces:

In regard to the foundation of the People's Revolutionary Party of South Vietnam, the creation of this party is only a matter of strategy; it needs to be explained within the party; and, to deceive the enemy, it is necessary that the new party be given the outward appearance corresponding to a division of the party (*Lao Dong*) into two [parts] and the foundation of a new party . . .

Within the party, it is necessary to explain that the founding of the People's Revolutionary Party has the purpose of isolating the Americans and the Ngo Dinh Diem regime, and to counter their accusations of an invasion of the South by the North. It is a means of supporting our

---

[20] Department of State, *Aggression from the North*, Washington, D.C.: Government Printing Office, 1965, pp. 22, 23.

sabotage of the Geneva agreement, of advancing the plan of invasion of the South, and at the same time permitting the Front for Liberation of the South to recruit new adherents, and to gain the sympathy of non-aligned countries in Southeast Asia.

The People's Revolutionary Party has only the appearance of an independent existence: actually our party is nothing but the *Lao Dong* Party of Vietnam . . . unified from North to South under the direction of the Central Executive Committee of the party, the chief of which is President Ho. . . .

During these explanations, take care to keep this strictly secret, especially in South Vietnam, so that the enemy does not perceive our purpose.

Do not put these explanations in party bulletins. . . .[21]

Although one must assume that not every Viet Cong operation in the field is checked out with the top Party and military echelons in Hanoi prior to execution, there is preponderant evidence in the public record of statements and action that the basic policies and their execution are guided by the Northern directorate.

In a later period, Communist journals in both North and South openly confirmed the direction of the Southern revolutionary effort and its tactics by the *Lao Dong*. As *Hoc Tap* commented in its September 1966 issue:

On the basis of keeping firm in strategy, our Party cleverly applied its tactics: On the one hand, it cleverly took advantage of the regional and temporary contradictions of the enemy to sow division among him. On the other hand, it united with anyone who could be united, won over anyone who could be won over, neutralized anyone who should be neutralized, completely isolated the imperialists and their

---

[21] *Ibid.,* p. 57.

more dangerous lackeys, and concentrated the spearhead of attack on them to overthrow them.

The policy of founding the Indochinese Democratic Front between 1936 and 1939, the Viet Minh Front and the Lien Viet Front between 1941 and 1951; the decision to sign the 6 March 1946 preliminary accord; the present NFLSV policy of upholding the mottoes of independence, democracy, peace and neutrality, and so forth, are typical examples of the clever application of the . . . instruction of Lenin. . .

Or as the *Liberation Army* newspaper in the South expressed it on February 2, 1967 in connection with the 37th Anniversary of the Vietnam Workers Party (*Lao Dong*):

. . .The northern troops and people have wholeheartedly helped the anti-U.S. national salvation resistance of the southern troops and people. . . . Under the National Liberation Front leadership the southern liberation forces have been built and developed along the leading principles and the experiences of the Vietnam People's Army. It is precisely this leadership which is the decisive factor. . . . On the occasion of this happy anniversary day the southern liberation armed forces enthusiastically and respectfully offer their deepest gratitude and warmest greetings to the Vietnam Workers Party which has led our people in rising up and struggling for independence and freedom and is leading our people in advancing firmly and achieving glorious victories in our era. The southern liberation armed forces respectfully offer their boundless confidence, love and respect to President Ho, leader of the Vietnam Workers Party and of our nation. . . .

Truong Chinh expressed the idea of *Lao Dong* Party leadership as a cardinal matter of doctrine in an interview reported by the Vietnam News Agency on January 11, 1967:

. . .There must be a Marxist-Leninist Party to give unified leadership to the revolutionary struggle of the people, lead the people from the national democratic people's revolution to the socialist revolution. This Party must . . . work out a correct political program to lead the whole revolution in its country. . . .

Northerners or Southern personnel trained in the North dominate the hard core of the Viet Cong fighting units which bear the brunt of the military actions. This fact has been amply documented by statistical compilations and case studies published by the South Vietnamese Government and the United States Government. Combat operations of United States and Vietnamese troops have turned up the same evidence again and again, as have the interrogations of Viet Cong prisoners and defectors. The lower-level provincial and village part-time guerrillas are largely indigenous Southerners (although many are simply coerced into service), but the real punch of the Viet Cong is provided by the men Hanoi knows are its own. As the supply of native Southerners trained in the North has decreased through casualties and has been shown to be inadequate to the demands of larger-scale military operations, massive infiltration of several divisions of the regular army of North Vietnam (the PAVN) has taken place over the past two years.

Military infiltration case histories from the February 1965 White Paper illustrate the two sources of Hanoi-controlled military personnel. First, the story of a Southerner trained in the North and sent back to South Vietnam:

Tran Quoc Dan was a VC Major, commander of the 60th Battalion . . . he surrendered to the authorities in South Vietnam on February 11, 1963.

At the age of 15 he joined the revolutionary army (Viet Minh) and fought against the French forces until 1954 when the Geneva Accords ended the Indochina War. As a regular in the Viet Minh forces, he was moved to North Vietnam. He became an officer in the so-called People's Army.

In March 1962 Major Dan received orders to prepare to move to South Vietnam. He had been exposed to massive propaganda in the North which told of the destitution of the peasants in the South and said that the Americans had taken over the French role of colonialists. He said later that an important reason for his decision to surrender was that he discovered these propaganda themes were lies. He found the peasants more prosperous than the people in the North. And he recognized quickly that he was not fighting the Americans but his own people.

Two turning points in the character of the men infiltrated occurred in 1964. Prior to that year almost all of the men infiltrated were native Southerners who had been ordered north after 1954 and had received extensive military and subversive training. In 1964, with the apparent depletion of that pool of Southerners, at least one-half of the infiltrators were native North Vietnamese. As the White Paper stated:

. . . reports of infiltration by native North Vietnamese in significant numbers have been received in Saigon. . . . It is estimated that as many as 75 percent of the more than 4,400 Viet Cong who are known to have entered the South in the first 8 months of 1964 were natives of North Vietnam.

Vo Thanh Vinh was born in Nghe An Province in North Vietnam in 1936. He was captured by South Vietnamese forces on May 5, 1964. He described himself as a military security officer. He infiltrated into South Vietnam in April 1964 with a group of 34 police and security officers from the North.

Another native North Vietnamese captured in the South was VC Private First Class Vo Quyen. His home was in Nam Dinh Province. He was a member of the 2d Battalion of the North Vietnamese Army's 9th Regiment.

These reports destroy one more fiction which the authorities in Hanoi have sought so long to promote—that the fighting in the South was a matter for the South Vietnamese. They underline Hanoi's determination to press its campaign of conquest with every available resource.[22]

The second and more significant change took place as regular tactical units of the North Vietnamese army entered South Vietnam in late 1964, that is, prior to the United States bombing of North Vietnamese military targets which began in February 1965.

North Vietnam has also become the principal source of Viet Cong weapons and other materiel. During the earlier periods of the insurgency, the guerrillas depended largely on cached weapons and arms captured from the Army of the Republic of Vietnam (ARVN), but these sources became insufficient for the scale of operations to which the rebels were committed after 1963. The massive increase in deliveries from the North has been illustrated by the large dumps of weapons from North Vietnam captured during the last year or two. It should be pointed out that the Hanoi regime has received considerable military assistance over the years from both the USSR and China, that Peking is the original source of most of the armament infiltrated into the South, and that Moscow has given concrete expression of its support in furnishing MIG fighter aircraft and SAM systems to North Vietnam.

As early as 1962, after studying a great mass of evidence for some time, the International Control Commission made the following pertinent statement on Hanoi's role in its report of June of that year:

> . . . The Committee has come to the conclusion that in specific instances there is evidence to show that armed and unarmed personnel, arms, munitions and other supplies have been sent from the Zone in the North to the Zone in the South with the object of supporting, organizing and carrying out hostile activities, including armed attacks,

---

[22] Department of State, *op. cit.*, pp. 6, 11, 12.

directed against the Armed Forces and Administration of the Zone in the South. . . .[23]

Despite all the evidence, Hanoi leaders sometimes flatly deny various aspects of the North Vietnamese role, but usually with a touchily indignant air of moral outrage which gives the game away. This attitude is illustrated in part of the interview which Premier Pham Van Dong gave the American Communist theoretician, Herbert Aptheker, and Yale professor Staughton Lynd, in early 1966:

Question: If the U.S. withdrew its troops, would the DRV withdraw its troops from South Vietnam?

Answer: The so-called presence of forces of the Democratic Republic of Vietnam in South Vietnam is but a myth fabricated by the U.S. imperialists by way of justification for their war of aggression in South Vietnam.

Question: It is often said that the NFLSV is an agent of the DRV and that the DRV is controlled by the Chinese People's Republic. What is your reply?

Answer: This is a vile fabrication designed to slander the Vietnamese people, the NFLSV, the DRV and the CPR.[24]

On the whole, Hanoi has been far from shy about its all-out support of the Viet Cong. However, it has maintained the clandestine nature of its infiltration of personnel southward, and the leadership has been consistent in denying the presence of regular North Vietnamese Army units. These somewhat contradictory themes were both present in an interview

---

[23] Foreign Office, London. "Documents Relating to British Involvement in the Indo-China Conflict, 1945-1965." Cmnd. 2834, Her Majesty's Stationery Office, Dec., 1965, pp. 195-203.

[24] *Vietnam News Agency*, January 28, 1966.

which Ho Chi Minh granted in December 1965 to British writer Felix Greene:

Question: The Government of the United States says that the reason why North Vietnam is being bombed is to discourage you from helping the revolutionary forces in the South, and that the bombing would stop immediately if you would leave your neighbour alone. What do you have to say about this?

Answer: The U.S. Government has launched savage air attacks on the territory of the Democratic Republic of Vietnam, an independent and sovereign state. In so doing, it has grossly trampled underfoot international law, most seriously violated the 1954 Geneva Agreements on Vietnam, and flouted humanity and justice. . . .

            The contention that the southern part of our Fatherland is "a neighbour country" separate from the North is a misleading one. It is just like saying that the southern states of the United States constitute a country separate from the northern states.

Question: The United States says that it has in its possession overwhelming evidence of your support for the National Front of Liberation in South Vietnam—what we refer to as the "Viet Cong." They specifically refer to your 325th division and other units of your regular army that are fighting in South Vietnam. What help are you giving to the Viet Cong? What troops? What weapons? How many volunteers from North Vietnam have gone to fight in the South?

Answer: To fabricate false evidence in order to slander North Vietnam is a deceitful trick of the U.S. Government to cover up its aggression in South Vietnam. The truth is that the United States

and its satellites have brought in foreign troops
to wage aggression on South Vietnam, in contra-
vention of the 1954 Geneva Agreements. . . .
Vietnam is one, the Vietnamese people are one.
As sons and daughters of the same Fatherland
our people in the North are bound to extend
wholehearted support to the patriotic struggle
waged by the people of the South against U.S.
aggression . . .[25]

Hanoi's Peace Terms: Surrender of South Vietnam to Communism

North Vietnam has pursued its war objectives with a tenacity
and steadiness of purpose that reflect an austere and fanatic
devotion to its revolutionary cause. This inflexibility also
springs from an enviable position as a recipient of aid and
comfort from both China and the USSR and a sense of encouragement derived from evidences of disunity and divided counsel
in the enemy camp. Hanoi's dedication to the task is a mixture
of strong belief in the justice of its unification mission in Vietnam and a fairly confident belief that within the present param-
eters of military action it has the physical means to carry off the
spoils eventually. Ho Chi Minh realizes perfectly well that he
is the only Vietnamese leader widely known throughout the
whole country and that his nationalistic credentials go a long
way toward offsetting his Communist background. The small
inner group of men around him also know they are the strongest
cohesive political leadership in Vietnam. They are also aware
that despite their puny strength relative to the United States,
they can count on some significant assets. One is a tight and
austere regimentation and mobilization of the Northern populace which makes other Communist states, in Eastern Europe

---

[25] *Vietnam Courier*, No. 42, December 16, 1965, p. 1.

and elsewhere, look almost liberal by comparison; another is the strongest army in Southeast Asia, with a tradition of guerrilla warfare, which can be effectively fed into South Vietnam to bolster the Viet Cong almost indefinitely, so long as present combat rules remain in effect. Finally, there is confidence that the vast and pervasive Communist political and subversive structure within South Vietnam stands a good chance of surviving military setbacks.

Hanoi has also achieved a remarkably independent position and a notable freedom of action vis-à-vis the USSR and Communist China. By astute maneuvering in the rift between Moscow and Peking and by actual exploitation of the schism, the *Lao Dong* leadership has not only succeeded in obtaining the support of the Communist giants for its ambitions in Indochina, but has also fostered a rousing competition in furnishing the material assistance needed to realize these goals.

When North Vietnam looks beyond its borders, it is encouraged to continue the war not only by its exaggerated reading of disunity signs in the United States and by very solid evidence of a total lack of concern in much of the Free World over Hanoi's aggression, but also by the constant reminder that chronic political instability is a basic factor in South Vietnam. Knowing their own totalitarian party and police apparatus can survive almost any likely development, Ho and his inner circle have undoubtedly taken comfort in watching the quarreling factions in South Vietnam tear at each other's throats, even though the Viet Cong have been incapable of effectively exploiting this unrest. Some signs that this instability is diminishing do not as yet appear to have influenced Hanoi.

Therefore, North Vietnam has rejected all proposals for peace, except on terms which are a blueprint for surrender of South Vietnam to Communism. Hanoi's basic four-point policy on peace terms (or rather, what at the time of announcement seemed its preconditions for beginning peace talks) were laid down in a resolution by the National Assembly in April 1965:

1—Recognition of the fundamental national rights of the Vietnamese people: sovereignty, independence, unity and territorial integrity. In strict conformity with the Geneva Agreements, the U.S. Government must withdraw its troops, military personnel, weapons, ammunition and other war materials from South Vietnam, dismantle all U.S. military bases there, abolish its military alliance with the stooge administration in South Vietnam. At the same time, it must stop all acts of war against North Vietnam and completely end all acts of encroachment upon the territory and sovereignty of the Democratic Republic of Vietnam.

2—Pending the realization of peaceful reunification of Vietnam and while Vietnam is temporarily divided into two zones, the military provisions of the 1954 Geneva Agreements on Vietnam must be strictly respected: the two zones must refrain from joining any military alliance with foreign countries, there must be no foreign military bases, troops or military personnel in their respective territory.

3—The internal affairs of South Vietnam must be settled by the South Vietnamese people themselves in accordance with the program of the National Liberation Front of South Vietnam without any foreign intervention.

4—The realization of peaceful reunification of Vietnam must be settled by the Vietnamese people in both zones themselves, without foreign intervention.

The above stand constitutes the basis for the most correct political settlement of the Vietnam question. Only when this basis is recognized can there be favorable conditions to achieve a peaceful settlement on the Vietnam question. Only when this basis is recognized is it possible to consider the convening of an international conference of the type of the 1954 Geneva conference on Vietnam.[26]

---

[26] Hanoi: *Vietnam News Agency*, April 13, 1965.

Ho Chi Minh reiterated Hanoi's tough stand in a form letter to chiefs of state of Communist countries on January 24, 1966:

> Dear Comrade President: I have the honor to call your attention to the war of aggression waged by the U.S. imperialists in our country, Vietnam.
>
> It is crystal clear that the United States is the aggressor who is trampling underfoot the Vietnamese soil. The people of South Vietnam are the victims of aggression and are fighting in self-defense. If the United States really wants peace it must recognize the National Liberation Front of South Vietnam as the sole genuine representative of the people of South Vietnam and engage in negotiations with it.
>
> The Vietnamese people will never submit to the U.S. imperialists' threats.
>
> So long as the U.S. army of aggression still remains on our soil, our people will resolutely fight against it . . .[27]

On January 27, 1966, Hanoi Radio added commentary on the National Liberation Front as "sole" representative of South Vietnam:

> In his exposé of U.S. policy on television on 23 January 1966, U.S. Secretary of State Dean Rusk once again brazenly declared that the Viet Cong are only one political element in South Vietnam and that as long as the demand remains that the Viet Cong play the principal role in South Vietnam, peace prospects will remain dim.
>
> To fight and defeat the U.S. imperialists, the South Vietnamese people must have a political organization to provide leadership. . . . Such an organization is the National Front for the Liberation of South Vietnam. Born more than five years ago, the front has clearly displayed its political prestige and obvious power. The front has gained control of four-fifths of South Vietnamese territory and 10

---

[27] *Vietnam News Agency*, January 28, 1966.

million people. . . . The front's stands and policies have always been carried out voluntarily by the broad masses of people. . . . The front has official representations in 11 countries. The front banner has flown on the five continents—and even in the United States.

From the political, legal, and sentimental viewpoints, it is clear that the National Front for the Liberation of South Vietnam is the sole genuine representative of the South Vietnamese people. As the only genuine representative of 14 million people of South Vietnam, the National Front for the Liberation of South Vietnam is fully entitled to settle the internal affairs of the South Vietnamese in accordance with the front program. . . .

It is clear that the important "rider" in all proposals by Hanoi to return to the provisions of the 1954 Geneva Accords is the insistence that the Viet Cong be recognized as the sole representative of South Vietnam and that its political program be accepted as the only proper solution to the Vietnam problem. This point, which is really what the war is all about, has nothing whatsoever to do with the Geneva Accords. That agreement had inadequate enforcement machinery and was a veritable "sieve" through which Hanoi could perpetrate several types of indirect aggression against the other Indochinese states, but at least it had no provision for automatic absorption of all Vietnam by the Communist regime in the North or its Southern protégés.

Hanoi has not limited itself to rebuffing U.S. peace talk feelers as a "hoax and swindle." It has also rejected peace overtures by outside parties, such as the British Commonwealth, the non-aligned nations, Pope Paul, the United Nations, and others. On the Declaration of the 17 Non-Aligned Nations, Hanoi had this to say:

On March 15, 1965, the representatives of a number of non-aligned countries, meeting in Belgrade, expressed deep concern over the increasingly serious situation in Vietnam, holding that "this is the consequence of the interference of foreign countries," and called on parties concerned to hold negotiations as soon as possible and without preconditions in order to find a political solution to the Vietnam problem . . .

To settle the Vietnam problem at present, the only correct way is to carry out the points laid down by Premier Pham Van Dong of the DRV on April 8, 1965.

This stand unquestionably enjoys the approval and support of all peace and justice-loving governments and peoples in the world. . . . Any approach tending to secure a United Nations intervention in the Vietnam situation is also inappropriate, because such approaches are basically at variance with the 1954 Geneva Agreements on Vietnam.

Among the 17 countries which sent representatives to the meeting held in Belgrade on March 15, 1965, some did not sign the appeal issued by this meeting. Others who signed it because they were not accurately informed about the bloody war provoked in South Vietnam by the United States imperialists and the latter's piratical attacks against the Democratic Republic of Vietnam, have now shown unwillingness to support that appeal. . . .

The Vietnamese people are resolved to use their legitimate right to self-defence, fulfil their sacred duty to defend their independence, sovereignty, unity and territorial integrity, and, at the same time, contribute to the struggle for the victory of peace, national independence, democracy and social progress of the world's people as a whole.[28]

The official *Lao Dong* journal was considerably less polite in rejecting a proposed British Commonwealth peace mission to Hanoi and other capitals which would explore chances for negotiations:

---

[28] Foreign Office, London. "Recent Exchanges Concerning Attempts to Promote a Negotiated Settlement of the Conflict in Vietnam." Cmnd. 2756. Her Majesty's Stationery Office, 1965, pp. 63-65.

What, in essence, is Wilson's so-called peace initiative?

. . . BBC said on June 18: "It is certain that British Prime Minister Harold Wilson would not have proposed the five-Premier mission to the Commonwealth conference without prior consent from the USA. . . ." Meanwhile, the Vietnamese traitors in Saigon also welcomed this proposal and promised that they would heartily welcome the mission.

These facts clearly show that Wilson's so-called peace initiative is but an intrigue already approved by the USA, aimed at realising the US aggressors' scheme to carry out their peaceful negotiation swindle while continuing to intensify their aggressive war.

The Wilson Government has been actively serving Johnson in this swindle . . .

Wilson's intrigue can be seen more clearly in the tasks he assigned to the mission he led. As defined in the communique already published, this mission does not name U.S. imperialism as the war provocateur, does not demand that the U.S. aggressors withdraw from South Vietnam and put an end to the acts of war against North Vietnam, completely ignores the existence of acts of war against North Vietnam, and completely ignores the existence of the SVNLF, the sole authentic representative of the South Vietnamese people. . . .

This undertaking is nothing other than a scheme to help the U.S. aggressors out of their stalemate and cover up their new criminal acts. . . .[29]

Pope Paul's efforts at year-end 1965 met with this intransigent reply from Ho Chi Minh:

I have the honor to acknowledge receipt of your message and wish to extend my thanks for the interest you show in the problem of peace in Vietnam.

---

[29] *Ibid.*, pp. 92-95.

The Vietnamese people eagerly want peace to reconstruct their country, but genuine peace is inseparable from genuine national independence.

The aggression by the American imperialists against Vietnam is the deep origin and direct cause of the present war in Vietnam. . . .

The U.S. leaders want war and not peace. The talks about unconditional negotiations made by the U.S. President are merely a maneuver to cover up his plan for war intensification and extension in Vietnam.

Let the U.S. put an end to its aggression, then peace will immediately be restored in Vietnam.

The Vietnamese people and the Government of the Democratic Republic of Vietnam sincerely thank the people of the world for their warm support of the Vietnamese people against the U.S. imperialist aggressors. . . .[30]

In February, 1966 the North Vietnamese Foreign Ministry barely gave the United Nations the time of day, brusquely rejecting the legitimacy of any initiative on the Vietnam War by the world organization:

. . . As on previous occasions, this time the United States is again seeking to use the U.N. organization to cover up the expansion of the war of aggression in Vietnam and to force on the Vietnamese people a settlement of the Vietnam question according to U.S. terms.

The government of the Democratic Republic of Vietnam reaffirms once again that on the international plane, the consideration of the U.S. war acts in Vietnam falls within the competence of the 1954 Geneva conference on Indochina and not the U.N. Security Council. Any resolution

---

[30] *The New York Times,* December 30, 1965. A further peace initiative by the Pontiff in early 1967 elicited a similar and equally adamant rejection by Hanoi.

by the U.N. Security Council intervening in the Vietnam question will be null and void.[31]

By late 1966 and early 1967, some signs were appearing that Hanoi might be shifting its ground somewhat in connection with possible peace talks. It had never been clear that the North Vietnamese leaders intended the "four points" of 1965 to be absolute preconditions for commencing negotiations. The evidence has more clearly indicated these actually to be Hanoi's agenda for negotiations, which were extended initially as bargaining points for the purpose of arranging peace talks, should such talks seem desirable. The tone of some of Premier Pham Van Dong's statements to *The New York Times'* correspondent Harrison Salisbury on January 2, 1967, is illustrative:

Now we come to the big question—the prospects of the war. How long will the war last? In this connection we are preparing for a long war because a people's war must be a long war. A war against an aggressor has to be a long war. . . .

That is why we are preparing for a long war. How many years? Ten, 20—what do you think, about 20?

. . . how many years the war goes on depends on you, not on us.

For us a settlement is a very simple question. As far as we are concerned, a war of aggression is a colonial war, an unjust war.

So a settlement is to stop it.

This kind of logic is flawless and irrefutable. Do you agree?

Now the best solution is that the Americans stop their war of aggression. The whole problem lies in that. . . .

[31] *Vietnam News Agency*, February 1, 1966.

. . . We do not think of humiliating the United States. The United States is a big power. America respects its own honor. But we also respect our honor, and the moment the United States rulers put an end to the war, we will respect each other and settle every question. Why don't you think that way? We have our point of view and we have put forward four points which constitute a basis for settlement of the Vietnam question. These should not be considered "conditions."

They are merely truths . . .

. . . The ruling circles of the United States do not like to accept our four points, and particularly the third point. That means that they are still clinging to South Vietnam. . . .

Besides the four points we have also put another point. That is to demand that the United States put, unconditionally and for good, an end to bombing and all hostile activity against the North. . . .

. . . Now I want to talk to you about South Vietnam and the reunification problem. Concerning South Vietnam, we think the political program of the NLF is a very sound program—for independence, democracy, peace, neutrality. . . .

. . . Since the National Front is the clear-sighted leader of the struggle of the people, it has won warm support, it is now the only genuine representative of the people of South Vietnam. I must say the American ruling circles are very short-sighted in not admitting the situation. . . .

We have made public many times our position. So did the NLF. We must be reunified. There is no force in the world which can divide us. Because we are a united nation. I am from the South myself.

How will reunification happen? On the basis of independence and democracy. By peaceful means. The two parts of the country will have to discuss together as between brothers what is the best way, by which means, and through which stages reunification has to be carried out. There are many misunderstandings. People say we will annex the South. We are not going to do this stupid, criminal act. We deeply respect the feelings of our brothers in South Vietnam. That is why we are supporting each other and uniting our strength in the fight against the common enemy. . . .

. . . That is why we say we must be reunified, but we will settle this among ourselves. We will consider the situation, what is the most convenient means, and there is no haste in doing it. . . .[32]

A few weeks later Foreign Minister Nguyen Duy Trinh made a statement seemingly indicating that the only precondition necessary to negotiations was unconditional and permanent cessation of U.S. bombing of the North. However, none of all this apparently shifting attitude has been accompanied by any sign that Hanoi would be willing to reciprocate a U.S. bombing cessation with any act of de-escalation on its part. It is difficult to tell whether the North Vietnamese leaders really are attempting to get negotiations underway on favorable terms or have merely launched a campaign to build up world pressures which would force a termination of the bombing, now that it is beginning to hurt the North Vietnamese economy and war effort seriously.

North Vietnam will talk peace when its leaders are convinced that it is to their advantage to do so, when they have decided that their cause will be better promoted by political than by military means. No one can say with any certainty when this will be. It probably will not happen until Hanoi has gone through several more assessments, in Marxist terms, of the "objective situation." Whenever it does come, however, this decision will not mean that the contest for Vietnam will be over. For the

---

[32] *The New York Times,* January 8, 1967, p. 34.

Communist doctrine of "struggle" is the politics of perpetual warfare. Goals are constant; the means to attain them are variable.

Opposition in the United States Encourages Hanoi

Much discussion and debate have taken place over the extent to which the North Vietnamese are encouraged in their refusal to talk peace by opposition within the United States to American policy in Vietnam. No one knows, of course, what is really going on in the minds of the *Lao Dong* leadership. How much of Hanoi's exuberant comment on protests in the United States is purely propagandistic, or how strongly it reflects a genuine reassurance, cannot be judged with real accuracy.

Historical experience would tend to increase the optimism of Ho and the Politburo. They probably remember that the military battles won by the Viet Minh in 1946-54 were less important than the political and psychological defeats suffered by the French at home. Confidence that the enemy will be discouraged by the Maoist "laws" of revolutionary war also tends to give real importance to what Hanoi sees as a great international wave of protest against "imperialism." Finally, the patience on which Asian Communists claim a monopoly, combined with awareness of the American tendency to be restive, undoubtedly gives the North Vietnamese some well-founded hope that they can outlast their opponents in a protracted conflict.

The media in North Vietnam have given an inordinate amount of attention to dissent in the Free World, displaying an almost lyrical tone in reporting and analyzing protests and demonstrations in the United States. Much of this can be dismissed as inconsequential in assessing the views of the Hanoi inner circle on the importance of these events.

However, Premier Phan Van Dong addressed the National Assembly in April, 1965 in a more thoughtful vein, suggesting a genuinely hopeful attitude about such dissent:

> What causes us to be moved and enthusiastic is that in recent months, in the United States itself, a movement has been developing widely to oppose the U.S. imperialists who are stepping up the war of aggression in South Vietnam and increasing their acts of war against North Vietnam. This movement includes a great number of American people from all walks of life—workers, youth, women, students, intellectuals, religious people, congressmen, and journalists. The struggle forms have gradually become stronger and more abundant.
>
> Dear comrade deputies of the National Assembly, the anti-U.S. struggle of our people has received never-before-seen sympathy and wide support from the people in the world, . . . This is an event having international meaning of great importance. . . .[33]

During the interview with Felix Greene, cited earlier, Ho Chi Minh was moved to appeal to the American people in the following terms, indicating his gratification at opposition on the U.S. home front, as well as his refusal to recognize its limitations:

> Question: President Ho, our time is almost up. You have heard of the protest movement in the United States and judging by your newspapers here I think the scope and influence of this movement is being greatly exaggerated here. The great majority of the people of the United States support President Johnson. I am not an American but have lived there for many years. I believe Americans are essentially a well-intentioned and humane people. Have you any spe-

---

[33] Hanoi Radio, Domestic Service, April 13, 1965.

cial message you might like to send to the people of the United States?

Answer: As you have just said, the American people are essentially well-intentioned. That is why the great majority of the American people cannot support President L. Johnson's policy of aggression. . . . It is because of their love of justice and humanity that many progressive Americans from all walks of life, hundreds of thousands of youths, students, professors, scientists, lawyers, writers, artists, clergymen, and working people have courageously raised their voices and staged huge demonstrations against the Johnson Administration's policy of aggression in Vietnam. For their part the American youth resolutely refuse to be sent to Vietnam as cannon-fodder for the U.S. imperialists.

Our people highly value this struggle of the American people. . . .

I take this opportunity to extend our sincere thanks to the American people who are resolutely fighting for the cessation of the U.S. Government's war of aggression in Vietnam. U.S. imperialism is the common enemy of our two peoples. With our united struggle, it will certainly be defeated. Our peoples will be victorious.[34]

The Other Side of the Coin:
Hanoi Sometimes Faces Reality

North Vietnam's rejection of peace bids is usually accompanied by a great volume of propaganda on largely imaginary

---

[34] *Vietnam Courier, op. cit.,* p. 2.

Viet Cong victories. This output is apparently intended to communicate to both Vietnamese and outsiders that there is a solid basis in the military situation for perseverance on the course long set. It is difficult to say to what extent it is self-deluding to the leadership or based on erroneous reporting from the field.

However, despite the avowed determination of the Hanoi leadership to fight until victory, the realities of the situation facing them since the beginning of the massive American military commitment in February 1965 have apparently begun to make some impression. This growing understanding of the grim problems arising from the air attacks in the North and the tremendous firepower disposed by the United States in the South has been showing up in certain pronouncements to the Party elite and cadre elements, particularly since early 1966.

In the following portion of an article in the January 1966 political and theoretical journal *Hoc Tap,* General Vo Nguyen Giap expressed some sense of realism on the U.S. plan of operations in Vietnam and the military problem which this plan poses for the Communists:

> Obviously, the U.S. imperialist war of aggression has entered a new stage, the main characteristic of which is that in this war of aggression U.S. imperialism relies not only on the puppet troops and puppet regime as a main instrument, but also on the American expeditionary forces, whose numbers are growing steadily.

> The rebel army [Ed. note: the ARVN], supported by the strength of the U.S. expeditionary troops, is an important and indispensable force for the war of aggression and at the same time is a mobile force on the battlefield and a main force for pacifying and controlling and oppressing the people.

> Furthermore, it is a political buttress for the U.S. expeditionary forces. . . .

The U.S. imperialists hope that by pouring their expeditionary troops into South Vietnam they can build up a new, triple supremacy:

(1) to have their strategic mobile force strengthened,
(2) to consolidate their military bases in important strategic points,
(3) and to double the strength of their air force.

With this triple supremacy, they would carry out their plot to mount new attacks to wipe out the South Vietnamese people's revolutionary armed forces, maintain a firm position, or send more troops to occupy important strategic positions, and then rely on them to intensify the pacification in important areas and attack the liberated areas. They would try to control and oppress the masses of people, reoccupy a number of lost areas, encircle and isolate the southern battlefield, and intensify the war of destruction against North Vietnam in order gradually to gain the initiative and to settle the war in a manner favorable to them, while at the same time laying the foundation for any further expansion of their aggressive war whenever necessary.[35]

Shortly after, *Lao Dong* Politburo member Le Duc Tho discussed the problem of maintaining morale within the Party in the face of difficulties. His guidance, disseminated to higher Party echelons, took the form of warning, criticism, and exhortation. He made a rather intriguing assessment of the difficulties faced by Hanoi, which suggests that it is not easy to maintain monolithic Party unity in the face of adversity:

The difficulties experienced previously were not yet the greatest ones. The closer the enemy gets to destruction, the more madly it will writhe. Our entire Party must, therefore, be adequately prepared ideologically to cope with all eventual changes in the situation and with all plots

---

[35] *Hoc Tap,* January 1966.

and tricks of the enemy so that we can vanquish the U.S. aggressors under all circumstances. . . .

Faced with great changes in the situation and with the revolutionary tasks, a small number of comrades have developed erroneous thoughts and views. Concerning the combat task, they have made an incorrect assessment of the balance of power between the enemy and us and of the enemy ruses. Now, they entertain subjectivism and pacifism, slacken their vigilance, and fail to get ideologically ready for combat. Now, they see only difficulties and do not see opportunities; display pessimism, perplexity, and a reluctance to protracted resistance; fail to realize clearly the deceptive peace negotiation plot of the enemy; and rely on outside aid.[36]

Decay in Hanoi's confidence became evident in the late summer and autumn of 1966, as problems of morale and security were discussed more frequently in the North Vietnamese media. Newspapers complained of cadres who "wavered" and army men with "negative thoughts." Spy scare reports on Hanoi radio seemed to indicate that espionage efforts from the South were achieving some success. Ho Chi Minh himself addressed a conference of the People's Security Forces in October 1966 in the following vein:

. . . To frustrate all schemes of the enemy war of destruction, we must pay attention to defeating all enemy espionage and psywar activities, promptly preventing and suppressing all schemes of the reactionaries, satisfactorily protecting leading organs, armed forces, communication lines . . . and firmly maintaining discipline and security in North Vietnam. . . . It is necessary to strengthen further the task of taking action against evildoers and guarding secrets. . . .

---

[36] *Hoc Tap,* February 1966.

> Generally speaking, people's security officers and men are
> good, absolutely loyal to the party and people, and worthy
> of the confidence of the party and people. . . . However,
> in all units and organs you must be sincerely united, must
> completely eliminate individualism, must thoroughly cor-
> rect . . . overbearing manners, and must establish good
> relations between the security forces and the people.
>
> . . . Constant, correct criticism and sincere self-criticism
> must be carried out in order to help one another progress
> . . .[37]

In view of the heavy and continual American air attacks on
the North Vietnamese communications lines, a conference con-
vened by the Directorate General of Political Affairs of the
Military Transportation Service was a significant development
in early September of 1966. It was reported that the conference
reviewed the "political tasks" of the Service after a year under
American bombardment. The Director of Political Affairs made
the following comment at the meeting:

> It is necessary to grasp firmly the task of ideological guid-
> ance, concentrating on building the determination to
> accomplish successfully all duties and insure the flow of
> transportation in any circumstance of the war.
>
> It is necessary to grasp and understand thoroughly the
> policy and outlook of the people's war and the party in
> all tasks of our military transportation service.
>
> It is necessary to move further into the field of guidance
> . . . and to improve labor efficiency and quality.
>
> It is necessary to lead and insure the spiritual . . . activi-
> ties of the troops regularly.
>
> It is necessary to get hold of and strengthen the party's
> . . . leadership on the . . . transportation front.[38]

[37] Hanoi Radio, October 22, 1966.

[38] Hanoi Radio, September 12, 1966.

When considering the effects of Allied military pressure and erosion of Communist morale on Hanoi's decision for peace talks, it must be remembered that the decision will be based not on a negative assessment by the *Lao Dong* leaders of how badly they are being hurt, but on a positive estimate of how much more they will gain by shifting to the "political struggle" than by continuing the "armed struggle." Adverse military developments and lowered morale will be factors in this decision, but they will not be the decisive ones. The decision will be rationalized in Marxist-Leninist terms as advancing the revolution, and in these terms the explanation will not be insincere.

Ho Chi Minh's Longer View: North Vietnam's Wider Ambitions

In making an evaluation of Hanoi's position in the Vietnam War, it would be well to remember that the Communist leaders do not view the struggle entirely from the standpoint of North Vietnam's immediate objective of destroying the southern republic and reunifying the country. They also consider the war to have larger international significance in a Marxist-Leninist sense. Furthermore, there is a direct relationship between Hanoi's war in South Vietnam and North Vietnam's wider ambitions in Southeast Asia.

When *Lao Dong* spokesmen discuss the struggle in terms of ideology and the strategic needs of the socialist "camp of peace," they describe Hanoi as playing a "vanguard" role in the great "struggle against world imperialism," and especially as the "spearhead" of the effort to expel "United States imperialism" from Southeast Asia.[39] North Vietnam, of course, is

---

[39] A valuable study of larger Hanoi objectives is Justus M. Van der Kroef's "The War Seen from Hanoi," in *Vietnam Perspectives,* Vol. 1, No. 3, February 1966, pp. 22-31.

the only Marxist-Leninist state in Southeast Asia and considers itself both the defender of the frontier of Communism in that part of the world as well as the engine of its expansion. The journal *Hoc Tap* pointed out in September of 1966 that "our country is the focal point of the acute contradictions that exist in the world" and stated that the strategic and tactical knowledge gained in the war would be "useful to the revolutionary struggle of the people of the world." In this context, Hanoi firmly rejects proposals from the outside world that *all* Vietnam be neutralized as part of a peace settlement. A temporary neutralization of the southern half is not totally dismissed, but Hanoi makes quite clear that North Vietnam is a member of the Communist camp and will remain so.

Related to this larger Marxist-Leninist view is the relationship between the war and Ho Chi Minh's more specific objectives in the neighboring states. Hanoi naturally does not spell these out, but history and recent experience lead to the conclusion that aggressive designs against Laos, Cambodia and Thailand are part of North Vietnam's planning. The Vietnamese have historically been vigorously expansionist, and in the not too distant past imperial Vietnam was making a bid for control of the other Indochinese states. Only the arrival of the French in the 19th century prevented the absorption of Cambodia by the Vietnamese, and the same period was marked by a Vietnamese contest with the Thais over control of the decrepit kingdoms in Laos, which was also settled by the French.

When Ho Chi Minh organized an Indochina Communist Party in the 1930's, he was ostensibly planning for the mobilization of the revolutionary energies of all the French territories against the colonial master. At the same time, he knew that the Vietnamese Communists would control the movement, and he undoubtedly calculated that the ultimate victory would find his Party in a dominant position in Laos and Cambodia as well as Vietnam. As Politboro member Truong Chinh wrote in his 1946 book, *The August Revolution:* "The Vietnamese revolution . . . strongly promotes the liberation of Laotian and Cambodian peoples and other colonial countries in Southeast Asia." The Viet Minh did indeed make large incursions into Laotian territory during the anti-French war and were quite active in Cambodia as well. However, the "half a loaf" results at Geneva deprived Ho of some of these potential spoils. It has been reported that pressure from both the Chinese and Soviets at Geneva was necessary to bring withdrawals of the Viet Minh from Cambodia and from all but two provinces of Laos.

North Vietnam has since been active in making good some of these losses. Laos has been the scene of conflict almost uninterruptedly since 1954. A native Communist movement, the *Neo Lao Hak Xat* (NLHX) with its army, the Pathet Lao, has seized over half of the kingdom from the Royal Government at Vientiane. Several attempts to integrate this movement into a neutralist national government have failed. From the outset, Hanoi has been the guiding force, both politically and militarily, behind the NLHX, with its cadres providing the necessary discipline for the more easy-going Laotians. Attacks by the Communists in the 1959-1960 period and during and after the 1962 Geneva Conference on Laos yielded the territory which now protects the Ho Chi Minh Trail used for infiltration into South Vietnam, and increasing numbers of North Vietnamese Army troops have been reported in the Communist-held half of the country.

For a long time Souvanna Phouma, who has been the neutralist Prime Minister of Laos three times and is the dominant figure in Laotian politics, refused to recognize Hanoi's role publicly. However, since 1964, his neutralist credentials with Hanoi and Peking have been seriously damaged by his overt denunciation of North Vietnamese aggression in his country.

On Laotian Armed Forces Day, March 23, 1966, Souvanna had this to say:

> . . . During the past 16 years, our nation has fought a fierce war caused by the *Pathet Lao* and their supreme master, North Vietnam. . . . The aggressors have come from abroad. They are strong and superior in arms. This civil war, this cruel war, was premeditated by traitors who have brought in another regime to massacre our brother Laotians. . . . Because of the infiltration of troops and arms from North Vietnam into our kingdom, our armed forces have suffered losses. This proves that the *Pathet Lao* and North Vietnam have openly invaded our nation. . . .
>
> The fact that the aggressors have launched propaganda saying that our Laotian kingdom has become a foreign military base is a trick aimed at misleading the world. The enemy has launched this deceitful propaganda to conceal its dark schemes and to create conditions for stepping up aggression.

In a speech to the U.N. General Assembly on October 18, 1966, Prince Souvanna repeated his charges that North Vietnam has consistently violated the 1962 Geneva Agreements on Laos, used Laos as a base for aggression against South Vietnam and stationed entire battalions in Laos to attack Royal Government troops. He warned the U.N. "that the insidious process of wars of liberation" could lead to World War III "and engulf us all." This attitude and his granting of permission to the United States to bomb the Ho Chi Minh Trail have made Souvanna the object of vituperative and harshly threatening commentary from Hanoi. It would be most rash to predict that the non-Communist half of Laos would long survive a Viet Cong-Hanoi victory in South Vietnam.

It might be added that the Indian and Canadian members of the International Control Commission reported through the British Foreign Office on August 22, 1966 "convincing evidence of operations of North Vietnamese troops in Laos contrary to the 1962 Geneva Agreement."

Cambodia occupies an extremely uneasy position. Although Prince Norodom Sihanouk has kept himself in the good graces of both Peking and Hanoi by a neutralism consistently "leaning to the left," the Vietnamese Communists have not left his country alone. They constantly use Cambodian territory as sanctuary and for base camps during the fighting in South Vietnam. It is no longer a secret that up to two divisions of North Vietnamese Army troops are always in eastern Cambodia, in addition to thousands of Viet Cong guerrillas and main-force soldiers. Cambodia has had ample historical experience with the vigorous and aggressive Vietnamese, and its government must realize that the potential for permanent occupation by the Communist forces now in the country is very high. Sihanouk is probably quite realistic about ultimate Communist designs. His sometimes sycophantic gestures toward Hanoi and Peking may be interpreted in the light of his expressed determination to preserve the national and ethnic identity of the Khmers as long as possible and the implicit desire to put Cambodia and himself as low on the priority list for Communist absorption as possible.

Thailand is another target of North Vietnamese ambitions. As Thailand has been a traditional strong rival of the Vietnamese, this situation has historical roots. Bangkok's alliance with the United States through SEATO and bilateral arrangements has made her a special objective for both Peking and Hanoi. Both Communist China and North Vietnam are involved in the present Communist insurgency in Northeast Thailand, but Hanoi would be in the better position to capitalize on a victory in South Vietnam by moves in Thailand. Peking and Hanoi have organized and pledged support for the so-called "Thai Patriotic Front," a traditional Communist united front organization under whose banner guerrilla bands roam northeast Thailand, holding forced propaganda meetings, assassinating village chiefs, police and schoolteachers, and looting villages for supplies.

Basic training and infiltration channels for the Thai guerrillas are provided by the North Vietnamese. Captured and defected guerrillas have confirmed that the training and indoctrination center for this enterprise is at Hoa Binh, about 48 miles from Hanoi, and it is estimated that this center has produced up to 700 graduates since its establishment in 1961. Most of the guerrilla cadres are infiltrated into Thailand across the Communist-held part of Laos, and many of them are moved through the Communist-dominated Vietnamese minority in northeast Thailand which lives along the Mekong River. It can be safely assumed that Hanoi's support of the insurgency is something more than a mere "fraternal" gesture toward the Thai Communists.

Hanoi's posture contains all the dynamic elements of history, modern nationalism, international Communism and imperialist ambition. In analyzing the threat that North Vietnam poses to the peace and stability of Southeast Asia, all these complex factors must be carefully considered.

IV

The Viet Cong: Politics at Gunpoint

Much confusion surrounds the true nature and meaning of the Viet Cong movement. It has been described as a democratic political revolution or as one of the belligerent parties in a largely civil war. It has also been characterized more extravagantly as the engine of the unfinished Vietnamese revolution for national unity and independence, and some observers credit it with being a vehicle for social reform in a stagnant South Vietnamese community. While the Viet Cong movement partakes of these attributes to some degree, its essential characteristics are its designed role as the spearpoint of Hanoi's attempt to take South Vietnam by force and its subsequently inherited posture, proclaimed by Peking, as the vanguard of the strategy of "people's war."

Viet Cong Adaptation of "People's War" Doctrine to South Vietnam

As previously stated, the basic doctrinal and operational patterns of Viet Cong insurgency find their inspiration in Chinese and Viet Minh revolutionary experience. However, there are deviations and variations from the earlier models, as well as similarities. The differences should be stressed, as they define the truly distinctive elements of the Viet Cong contribution to what Marxists call "the rich treasury of revolutionary experience." These deviations occur in several categories: the circumstances surrounding the origin and development of the struggle in South Vietnam, the organization and leadership of the Viet Cong movement, operational doctrine, and the degree of genuine support the insurgents receive from the South Vietnamese people.

First, let us consider the origins and development of the present Vietnam war. In his theoretical framework for all aspects of revolutionary war, Mao Tse-tung sees the revolutionary armed forces going through three stages of warfare: (1) on the strategic defensive, (2) in a stalemate with the enemy who is gradually worn down by guerrilla attacks, and (3) passing from guerrilla operations to regular offensive warfare against the foe. Thus he pictures the "people's war" beginning with an all-out attack by the enemy against the revolutionary forces, the latter being thrown on the defensive for a considerable period of time. The enemy might be a foreign imperialist invader, a colonial occupier or the army of an intolerably "reactionary" indigenous government.

This Maoist model for the initiation of "people's war" did fit actual events of an earlier period in China and Indochina rather well. As the Japanese armies invaded China in the 1930's and the Nationalist armies of Chiang Kai-shek took the offensive against the Communist zones in the early 1930's and again after the Pacific War, the leftist forces were indeed initially on the defensive in a so-called "phase I" condition. This was also true of the Viet Minh guerrilla forces as the French Expeditionary Corps pushed vigorously to reoccupy Indochina for France after World War II.

The war in South Vietnam had a very different beginning, however. It was initiated by the guerrilla bands themselves, after a slow process of political penetration and subversion. As described in Chapter II, the Viet Minh leadership left considerable numbers of guerrilla cadres behind in the South after the Geneva partition. Although they operated underground whenever government pressure made it necessary, these elements conducted an effective Communist administration in large areas of the country where the Viet Minh had been strong, such as the provinces of Phu Yen, Binh Dinh, Quang Ngai and Ba Xuyen, and the areas north of Saigon and along the Cambodian border. Some foreign reporters who visited a few of these rural areas in the post-Geneva period were struck by the existence of established and apparently popular Communist local governments. In addition to these Viet Minh forces left behind in the "Red" zones, some tens of thousands of Southern Communist troops and sympathizers went North, later to become a source of reinforcement for the Viet Cong (as the Southern movement later came to be called). It was correctly calculated by the Northern authorities that these returnees would be accepted in their old native areas. Arms dumps were also cached for later use. Finally, a network of agents was left in the South which was to penetrate the police, armed forces and administration of the Saigon government, as well as many of the educational and economic enterprises.[40]

Gradually, the process of political penetration of the government areas went forward. The cadres began to infiltrate the lowland villages. They held propaganda meetings among the peasants, exploiting grievances the villagers strongly felt and developing some they were unaware of. As the landlords began

---

[40] Fairly detailed and informative accounts of the rather obscure period of the first five years after Geneva can be found in the numerous articles on Vietnam by Denis Warner which appeared in *The Reporter* and *The New Republic* during that period. Other excellent sources are: Bernard Fall, *The Two Viet Nams* (Praeger, 1964), Robert Scigliano, *South Vietnam: Nation Under Stress* (Houghton Mifflin, 1964) and Denis Warner, *The Last Confucian* (Penguin Books, 1964).

to return to the rural areas after the anti-French war to collect back rent, the issue of land tenure and rents took on great importance, and the Communists used it to the fullest. After indoctrination took hold with a few farmers in a village, the infection began to spread. Under the leadership of the Party cadres, farmers' associations were formed and expanded their membership rapidly.

Taking care of land problems and grievances against corrupt officials may well have ended the peasants' interest in the Viet Cong movement, except that the Communists had much broader plans for them. The "struggle" movement had to be propelled to greater strength and militancy, and the influence of the Diem government, which remained strong in many of the villages, had to be eliminated. Therefore, the Party began a campaign of measured violence against the village leaders and local security agents. Discriminate terror, which was to become such a striking feature of the Viet Cong movement, began by 1957 and reached alarming proportions by 1959, usually taking the form of assassination and kidnapping.

After the destruction of the Diem government's influence, many of the villages became in effect independent entities, administered by their own Communist regimes. But the peasants' interests still remained narrow and self-centered. They may have been pleased with the schools, sanitation facilities, first-aid stations and produce markets established by the Party, but they still lacked militant dedication to the "national liberation" struggle. While it cannot be documented in a cause-and-effect relationship, the dissatisfaction expressed in numerous captured Viet Cong reports with the shallowness of village spirit during those years indicated a lack of progress in the political war which may well have influenced Hanoi to order a shift to the "armed struggle" in 1959. At any rate, this change of direction soon resulted in marked expansion of the Viet Cong hold on the countryside.

At the same time as these Viet Cong activities took place in the ricelands, the Communists mounted a serious campaign to subvert the *montagnards* in the high plateau of central Vietnam. This area was to become one of the keys to the war, for it contained the termini of the infiltration trails through Laos and Cambodia. The primitive tribal peoples of the highlands have almost always been wretchedly treated by the lowland Vietnamese, and they were a vulnerable target for the Viet Cong, particularly as the Communists could point with some justification to the progress made by the tribal minorities in the North under Ho Chi Minh's administration. The Communists, by a combination of persuasion and terror, were sufficiently successful in the highlands to establish numerous base camps ready to receive the infiltrators from the North after the shooting war got under way in earnest.

Some writers (particularly the French) describe the Viet Cong's resort to violence as a necessary reaction to the unbearably brutal suppression campaigns carried out by President Ngo Dinh Diem. He did indeed take some harsh measures against the Communist elements, but his army and police never mounted an all-out offensive against the dissidents. First of all, the Communists were too well-entrenched in their long-occupied strongholds to be vulnerable to "mop-up" campaigns. Only in the contested areas did they suffer appreciable casualties. Second, Diem's forces never had the organization and resources to cope with the threat. Some of the reports from that period indicate that the President himself and a few of his senior military officers had a better understanding of the nature of the Communist strategy unfolding in the South Vietnamese countryside than did the American military and civilian personnel in Saigon, who seemed exclusively intent on producing a Vietnam-

ese Army that could meet a conventional invasion from the
North. Diem's requests for the kind of military and economic
aid that would effectively meet the challenge of rural revolt
apparently met little response. For this and other reasons,
the Self-Defense Corps and Civil Guard, upon whom the main
burden of rural security fell, remained pitifully untrained and
incompetent, as well as starved logistically.

Diem's harsh hand fell heaviest on the urban opposition and
educated elite of South Vietnam, not upon the Communists. As
his increasingly dictatorial and arbitrary methods alienated
more and more elements among the intellectual, political and
military leaders, some of them did join with the Communists
to form the National Liberation Front. However, those who
took this step were on the whole insignificant figures. Large
numbers of disaffected members of the Cao Dai and Hoa Hao
religious sects gave support to the NLF, but only until Diem's
death. However, most of the members of political opposition
groups remained clearly aware of the ultimate objectives of the
Viet Cong and refused them cooperation.

Of course, there is no profit in belaboring the issue of how
the shooting war started in terms of variation from the Maoist
model, for the Chinese leader has always been willing to make
allowance for differences in political, economic, and social
conditions in various countries and environments. But the
point is important in establishing the fact that, unlike their
predecessors in China and Indochina, the Communists in
South Vietnam did not have their war thrust upon them by
their opponents. *They* bear the responsibility for starting it.

Another variation in conflict origin and development from
the Chinese and Viet Minh models is the somewhat "foreign"
flavor which has colored the Viet Cong's war from the outset.
Although the majority of the Viet Cong have been Southerners, the presence of Northern cadres in the key positions

of leadership in the Viet Cong movement has been crucial. While Vietnam has certain attributes of a single nation, the spirit of regionalism and localism is very strong, and after 1954 the southern republic grew as a separate entity whose people pursued a remarkably prosperous course of development entirely different from their northern neighbors. Therefore, the hand of the "outsider" guiding the insurgency did not go unnoticed in the South. This is a sharp contrast to the earlier situation in revolutionary China and Indochina, where the popular struggle had almost entirely indigenous roots, and where the undoubted authenticity of the patriotic appeals of Mao and Ho attracted the loyalties of a large percentage of the population.

National Liberation Front: The Public Facade of the Viet Cong

In their political organization, which is traditional and very thorough, the Viet Cong show quite strong similarities to the Chinese Communist and Viet Minh models. This is true on both levels, the overt and the clandestine. In forming the National Front for the Liberation of South Vietnam (NLF) as their public political facade, the Viet Cong have used one of the most important elements of Maoist revolutionary strategy—the "united front." This concept expresses the need for non-Communist allies during the "anti-imperialist struggle," but the Viet Cong are careful to follow the Chinese precept that the Communist Party must have absolute domination from the outset. It is worth noting, however, that this leadership role of the Party is never as prominently publicized in South Vietnam as it was during the Chinese civil war. In fact, the NLF and its non-Communist titular leaders, who form the majority of its Central Committee, are allowed to monopolize the public spotlight and to give every appearance of directing the insurgency. It is perhaps for this reason that the NLF has become such a focus of controversy and confusion in the outside world over the issue of whether or not the Viet Cong movement is a genuine "home-grown" product.

This type of Communist Party alliance with certain non-Communist elements serves the useful purpose of deceiving the naïve and unwary both at home and abroad about the true nature of the war and disguising Communist control of the struggle. As a revolutionary device it has a respectably successful doctrinal base and historical experience. Lenin formulated the doctrine in a rudimentary way. The Chinese Communists used it to considerable advantage in the 1920's and again when the Japanese attack loomed in the 1930's. They repeated it with some of the minor anti-Kuomintang parties during the civil war of 1946-49 and, in fact, have continued to use this mechanism in their regime at Peking for whatever can be gained from it. Similarly, the Communists in Vietnam have used this gambit for 25 years, first to disguise their total control of the independence movement against the French—through the Viet Minh and Lien Viet front organizations—and later to camouflage their direction of the violent campaign to destroy South Vietnam.

Three months after the *Lao Dong* Party Congress of September 1960 had laid down the guidelines, the NLF was duly and officially promulgated from a Viet Cong base area in South Vietnam. In line with the deceptive impression it was designed to make, the Front's Manifesto studiously avoided Marxist slogans and terminology, emphasizing liberal democratic phraseology and programs. It was a ringing document, full of most attractive promises for virtually every segment of South Vietnamese society—high wages, low taxes, land to the tiller, essential democratic liberties, emancipation of women, social welfare, protection of private enterprise, a peaceful foreign policy, etc., etc. Understandably, the Manifesto did make a favorable original impression among some South Vietnamese who had become disenchanted with the increasingly arbitrary and repressive policies of the Ngo Dinh Diem regime.

The following portions of the Manifesto of the National Liberation Front illustrate the public language used by the organization to express its purported objectives:

> Overthrow the camouflaged colonial regime of the American imperialists and the dictatorial power of Ngo Dinh Diem, servant of the Americans, and institute a government of national democratic union. . . .

> Institute a largely liberal and democratic regime. . . . Elect a new National Assembly through universal suffrage.

> Implement essential democratic liberties: freedom of opinion, of press, of assembly, of movement, of trade-unionism; freedom of religion without any discrimination; and the right of all patriotic organizations of whatever political tendency to carry on normal activities. . . .

> Establish an independent and sovereign economy, and improve the living conditions of the people. . . .

> Support the national bourgeoisie in the reconstruction and development of crafts and industry. . . .

> Revitalize agriculture. . . .

> Institute a just and rational system of taxation. . . .

> Implement a labor code. . . .

> Organize social welfare. . . .

> Develop a national and democratic culture and education. . . .

> Liquidate illiteracy. . . .

Promote science and technology and the national letters and arts. . . .

Watch over public health. . . .

Establish a national army devoted to the defense of the Fatherland and the people; abolish the system of American military advisers.

Abolish the draft system. . . .

Abolish all foreign military bases established on the territory of Vietnam. . . .

Guarantee equality between the various minorities and between the two sexes. . . .

Promote a foreign policy of peace and neutrality.

Cancel all unequal treaties. . . .

Establish diplomatic relations with all countries . . .

Develop close solidarity with peace-loving nations and neutral countries. . . .

Stay out of any military bloc. . . .

Accept economic aid from any country willing to help us without attaching any conditions to such help.

Re-establish normal relations between the two zones, and prepare for the peaceful reunification of the country.

. . . The National Liberation Front of South Vietnam advocates the peaceful reunification by stages in conformity with the interests of the Vietnamese nation.

Struggle against all aggressive war; actively defend universal peace.[41]

Several years later, faced with a serious disruption of its timetable for takeover and a full American combat commit-

---

[41] Translation from Bernard Fall, *The Two Viet-Nams*, New York: Praeger, 1963.

ment in Vietnam, the Front was stating its goals more militantly, but essentially still without obvious Marxist vocabulary. However, the following portion of a statement of the NLF Central Committee on March 22, 1965 does make some public admission of liaison with Hanoi in the matter of weapons and personnel:

> Facing the present situation of utmost gravity, the South Vietnam National Front for Liberation deems it necessary to reaffirm once again its ironlike and unswerving stand to carry through the war of resistance against the U.S. imperialists.

> The heroic South Vietnamese people are resolved to drive out the U.S. imperialists in order to liberate South Vietnam, achieve an independent, democratic, peaceful and neutral South Vietnam, with a view to national reunification. . . .

> Vietnam is one, the Vietnamese people are one. North and South Vietnam are of the same family. . . . That the people in North Vietnam should be resolved to fulfil their duty toward their kith-and-kin in South Vietnam fully conforms to sentiment and reason. . . .

> The South Vietnam National Liberation Front has always relied mainly on its own strength and capacity, but it is ready to accept all assistance, both morally and materially, including weapons and all other war materials from all the socialist countries, the nationalist countries as well as all the international organizations and peace-loving people the world over. Besides, the front reserves for itself the right to buy weapons and war materials from other countries to strengthen the potentials of its self-defence war.

> If the U.S. imperialists continue to commit U.S. combat troops and those of their satellites to South Vietnam and continue to extend the war to North Vietnam and Laos, the South Vietnam National Liberation Front will call on the

peoples of various countries to send youth and army men to South Vietnam to side with the South Vietnamese people in annihilating the common enemy.

While the U.S. imperialists are constantly sowing suffering and death in South Vietnam, the South Vietnam National Liberation Front, if need be, cannot but call back the sons and daughters of South Vietnam, who have regrouped to the North in observance of the ceasefire agreement and who had to live far from South Vietnam during ten long years, to take arms to annihilate the enemy to save their country and families. . . .

The South Vietnamese people and their only genuine representative—the South Vietnam National Front of Liberation—will undoubtedly win final victory.[42]

The Clandestine Marxist Core: Engine and Pilot of the Revolution

Following the establishment of the NLF, Hanoi proceeded to construct the component parts of the Front. A Radical Socialist Party and a Vietnam Democratic Party, ostensibly non-Communist groups, were created out of whole cloth. They were and still remain largely paper organizations, showing little evidence of significant leadership, specific program or popular participation. However, one very genuine group was brought forward in 1962: the Communist Party of South Vietnam, formerly the Southern branch of the *Lao Dong,* now renamed the People's Revolutionary Party (PRP) for purposes of membership in the Front. While the PRP was avowedly a Marxist party, the purpose of the Communists was to appear as simply one of a number of diverse patriotic political groups banded together to oppose the oppressive Saigon government. In

---

[42] Hong Kong: *Hsin Hua* News Agency, *Selected News Items,* June 1965, pp. 1-5.

truth, the PRP was and is both pilot and engine of the revolution. The journal *Hoc Tap* in early 1966 not only painted a true picture of this position of the PRP but also exposed the real objectives of the NLF in frank and pointed language:

> The partisans of Marxism-Leninism are in fact the soul of the NLFSV. . . .

> The experiences of the world and our country's revolution have shown that in order to win the greatest success the national democratic revolution must be led by a workers' revolutionary party . . . The partisans of Marxism-Leninism in the South have clearly noted the need of a thorough revolutionary party to act as a vanguard force for the southern revolution . . .

> The PRP is a revolutionary party of the working class in South Vietnam, a Marxist-Leninist Party. It has applied in a creative manner the principles of Marxism-Leninism to the concrete situation of the South in order to set forth correct revolutionary policies, lines and methods . . .

> The PRP maintains that the revolutionary struggle of the southern people must necessarily use revolutionary violence of the masses to . . . advance toward smashing the reactionary government and replace it by a genuinely revolutionary government . . . Straying from this path can lead only to a failure.[43]

It is quite clear from this that the PRP is the organization which originates all plans and policies and thus controls the insurgency—not the NLF. This holds true from the top national echelons, through the regional, provincial and district hierarchies, and down to the hamlet level.

As in all Communist or Communist-dominated movements, both the National Liberation Front and the People's Revolu-

---

[43] Saigon: U.S. Mission in Vietnam, *The Communist Party of South Vietnam—A Study,* March, 1966 p. 8.

tionary Party are simultaneously political and military organizations in which the political arm controls the military. The Front has a Central Committee of 64 members with a small Presidium, as well as a number of overt subordinate committees dealing with political, military, social, economic, and external affairs. At the same levels the PRP Central Committee and its units operate as a control group within the Front headquarters.[44] As some of the NLF committees are designed as "shadow" ministries which would take over actual governmental functions at a suitable time, PRP domination of their activities assures Communist control of any future "liberation government."

Some feeling for the traditional Marxist-Leninist organization and operation of the People's Revolutionary Party can be gained in the following portion of a manual of rules for the Party captured in 1965 in South Vietnam:

Acceptance of new members

New prospective members must request acceptance and reveal their personal history to the Party for its examination.

They must be sponsored by two official members who are familiar with the background of each new prospective member.

Each prospective member must be investigated by every Party member in that cell.

The decision of the cell will be reviewed and must be approved by higher-ranking officers.

Each new member must go through a probationary period. . . .

---

[44] Douglas Pike, *Viet Cong, op. cit.* pp. 143-49, 210, 211, 217. This is a major and invaluable comprehensive work on the Viet Cong movement up to 1965.

Requirements for Prospective New Members

These are determined by the applicant's social and economic background.

Examples: Workers, farmers and poor people must be sponsored by two members who have been members for at least 3 months; workers must undergo a 3-month probationary period, farmers and poor people 4 months. Students and educated revolutionaries must be sponsored by 2 members who have been members for 9 months. Tribal minority people, whose class background cannot be determined, and ARVN personnel, must meet special requirements to be established. . . .

Party Organization

The Vietnamese People's Revolutionary Party is organized on the basis of democratic centralism. Work is to be given to each Party echelon and is to be carried out by each.

Party conference decisions must be made by majority opinion.

Before voting, each member has the right to speak his opinion; after voting all must obey the decision without question.

No organization of the Party can make any decision reserved to higher organs and cadres. . . .

Finance

Dues are paid by members and collected by the Party. Two-thirds go to higher echelons. The Central Committee must approve all fund-raising drives.[45]

In addition to the PRP and the two dummy non-Marxist parties, the Communists filled out the structure of the NLF

---

[45] Translation by Research Institute on Communist Strategy and Propaganda, University of Southern California, 1966. A marked similarity to the rules governing the Chinese and North Vietnamese parties is quite apparent.

with a large number of "liberation" associations allegedly representing in a functional way every significant social, economic, ethnic, religious, and professional group in South Vietnam. Actually many of these are groups with skeleton staff only, and there is little evidence of genuine voluntary public participation in them. However, there are some of them, particularly those for farmers and youth, which serve to enmesh the Vietnamese villages in an interlocking web of social and political pressures, both persuasive and coercive. These groups also usefully equate with similar international Communist front organizations, and by virtue of the publicity they receive at international gatherings, they appear more substantial and important than they really are.

Outside the vital military units, the truly significant Viet Cong organizations are not the well-publicized NLF and its baggage of national functional fronts, but rather the local hierarchies which carry out the essential daily functions of control and administration under the guidance of a hard core of dedicated and well-trained Marxist cadres. These offices and committees constitute the apparatus which makes the power and influence of the Viet Cong felt everywhere in the villages of a very large part of the country. They represent the ubiquitousness and pervasiveness of Viet Cong persuasion and coercion which impinge on the life of the peasant. In the areas controlled by the Viet Cong, they collect taxes, provide public services and mete out "justice," and in many contested zones they exercise these functions at night when Saigon's officials retire to the safety of the larger towns.

The Infrastructure: Struggle
At the Rice-Roots Level

The Viet Cong apparatus, or infrastructure, which permeates the rural areas of South Vietnam has frequently been described as the key to the survival or destruction of the movement. Vietnamese authorities feel that the primary and most difficult task in Vietnam is rooting out the tentacles of this omnipresent organization. Clearly, a basic knowledge of the role of the infrastructure in controlling the population is essential to an understanding of the war in Vietnam.

In describing the structure and its work on the provincial, district, village and hamlet level, it should be noted that the thousands of villages and hamlets of Vietnam, where Viet Cong activity is centered, do not fit the general Western concept or image of a village. They are not simply small settlements in one spot, but administrative organizations having numerous population clusters and often spreading over considerable areas. Some villages in South Vietnam have 12 to 16 hamlets and a population of up to 40,000, while individual hamlets may contain 2,000 or more inhabitants.

Although the infrastructure organization is not uniform, nor does it function in the same manner in all areas, the basic outlines can be delineated with reasonable accuracy. The Viet Cong have followed the general principle of centralization of policy-making and decentralization of execution. As one goes below the NLF Central Committee, which hands down the general directives for the movement under the guidance of its Marxist (PRP) core, the most important supervisory group is the provincial Central Committee. This body translates the over-all policies of the NLF Central Committee into more specific operational directives for the lower echelons. Its supervisory functions embrace: (1) direction of the political aspects of the war through orders to propaganda and *agit-prop* cadres and teams and by measures designed to keep the various village organizations properly motivated and active; (2) direction of the violence program, including both terrorism and military actions; and (3) regulation of training and indoctrina-

tion at various levels. The chairman of the provincial committee is most often a Communist, but not always. He pre-
sides over a body that may have from 100 to 200 members,
chosen to give the image of a broad spectrum of representation
from various social, functional, religious and ethnic groups.
There may be relatively few Marxists in the committee, but
they are the key members. There are varying numbers of
administrative and functional sections attached to provincial
headquarters, depending on the extent of Viet Cong strength
and activity in a particular province.

Next below the provincial level is the district committee,
which does not exist in all areas. It was the last echelon of
the structure to be formed by the NLF, considerably after
the provincial and village levels were organized. District committees are strongest in the western Delta region and Cambodian border area. There has been some question among
authorities on the Viet Cong as to the exact function of the
district echelon, but there is now widespread belief that it is
the most critical communications transmission link between
the provincial committee and the villages. It is probably the
most important lower-level base of the People's Revolutionary
Party and as such directly controls and manipulates the village
committees. Thus it constitutes the key connection between
operational directives and their execution. The district is
also considered to be the main echelon in the terrorist apparatus, with the district security group making important
decisions in the terror campaign. Most sabotage operations
in the countryside are carried out by district forces.

At the village and hamlet levels, the principal purpose and
function of the Viet Cong infrastructure can be most clearly
seen: controlling, mobilizing and directing the civilian population in support of the revolutionary war effort. Or as a
captured Viet Cong administrator's manual puts it:

> Our responsibility in the liberated area is to gather the
> people and rule them; to strengthen them politically, mili-
> tarily, economically, socially and culturally; to establish
> order and security; to improve the people's morality and
> material living conditions; to intensify the struggle against
> the enemy; . . . to mobilize manpower and resources
> so as to develop the revolutionary forces . . . and lay
> the foundations for a new political system. . . .[46]

Whereas the mobilization of the population in the earlier
years largely involved immediate political objectives, and still
does to a considerable extent in contested areas, the pressures
of the war have redirected the emphasis in the Viet Cong-
dominated areas to support of the combat forces through material means and manpower recruitment. Administrative personnel in the villages have come to concentrate on meeting
Viet Cong needs through taxation, food requisitions, intelligence collection and conscription.

As the village and hamlet organizations are largely civilian,
family-centered and locally oriented, they are not concerned
with the direction of the main force and regional military
units. The hierarchy at the village level is composed of the
NLF village administrative committee, a collection of village
"liberation" associations, functional mass organizations such as
the farmers' association, and the numerous individual cells
in the "liberation" associations. A village committee of 3 to 5
members might have a military cadre, a propaganda cadre, a
security cadre, and a finance cadre. Committee structure depends
largely on the local security situation. The village committee
chairman may or may not be a Party member, but the local **PRP**
chapter and its secretary hold the real levers of power at this

---

[46] Quoted in Pike, *op. cit.*, p. 287.

level. As a Viet Cong document on the village committee's functions states:

> As to leadership, it is advisable to allow members to select their own leaders . . . although key Party cadres should guide and obtain favorable representatives. . . .[47]

An individual peasant is recruited into a three-man cell, whose leader is a member of the hamlet cadre committee and, as such, is a key Party member in the rural areas. In fact the whole cell structure, which is really on a sub-hamlet level, is the most basic unit in the entire Viet Cong movement. The cell takes on an almost esoteric significance in Communist doctrine, for it is considered the primary cohesive element in the Party structure. It provides an effective means of mutual surveillance of its members and tends to ensure their loyalty and "revolutionary virtues."

The village and hamlet cadres are the hard-core energizers of the Viet Cong apparatus. They are the Party's representatives who make things move at the village level. Most cadres are natives of the village and well-known. Generally, a cadre does not work in the fields but is supported by the villagers and the Party while he occupies himself fully with organizational and operational matters. These duties are many and varied, including supervision of logistics, intelligence, communications and propaganda; leadership of guerrillas and youth groups; and tending to the care of battle casualties and to the solution of farmers' problems. The cadre is expected to be a paragon of behavior and devotion, and he gets all the blame when things go wrong.

The local guerrilla organization, as distinct from the Viet Cong Main Forces and North Vietnamese Army units, is the best trained and equipped group among the various categories

---

[47] *Ibid.*, pp. 224-225.

of Viet Cong irregulars. Because they are mobile and fairly well equipped, they have considerable operational flexibility. In addition to policing Viet Cong territory and providing protection for various types of Viet Cong activities, the guerrillas frequently act independently in harassing government outposts and performing acts of terrorism and sabotage. Also, they are frequently called upon to operate with Local Force units or as a reconnaissance screen for Main Force operations. Another category of irregulars, the self-defense force, consists primarily of older men and women and appears to perform a security and early-warning role. For example, when government forces approach a Viet Cong village, those on guard duty are expected to fire warning shots or sound some other tocsin, in order to allow the cadres to hide, either in holes or in nearby jungle. At the request of the village security cadre, they may also arrest persons for disciplinary action.

The total strength of the Viet Cong apparatus (i.e., excluding Main Force military units) has been variously estimated from 17,000 to 450,000, depending on one's definition of the infrastructure constituency. The larger figure includes all the guerrillas, the self-defense force, the porters and coolies, the couriers, and all the members of all the committees—in other words, all the "little brothers." A realistic estimate of the true activists in the apparatus would be much closer to the lower figure. It is estimated that a typical village counting 10,000 inhabitants would have an infrastructure strength, defined in fairly broad terms, of approximately 100.

A critical question in assessing the survival prospects of the Viet Cong is the extent to which this complex structure in the provinces is vulnerable to war pressures. At least until recently, the primitive but elaborate security system has been quite effective. Except in areas of strong Saigon government control, very little of the cadre structure has been underground, and although most villagers know who the cadres are, few know their emergency hiding places. Not until 1966 was there consistent government pressure on the villages sufficient to induce the wary and frightened peasants to give information or effective enough to create conditions tending to expose the Viet Cong apparatus. In contested areas, government police generally have known the identities of the NLF cadres, but they have either been powerless to act in the absence of government troops or have taken refuge in the claim that a Viet Cong must be caught in an overt act before he can be arrested. Some local pacts of "peaceful coexistence" might also be suspected.

A reversal of military fortunes since 1965 has now begun to expose some of the weakness of the infrastructure. Although it is difficult to predict how extensively this vulnerability may develop, the evidence is now clear from the Viet Cong defectors that the lower levels are prone to forsake the cause in the face of seriously adverse situations. The rapidly increasing numbers of defectors are coming from the popular functional groups, such as the farmers' associations, including some cadres at this level. At the lower echelons the degree of commitment to the NLF cause is not so great, and the family and community pressures on the individual are much greater than at the higher military and political levels, where an intense dedication has been coupled with an almost complete divorce from traditional personal and familial ties.

Whereas in earlier years anti-Viet Cong sweeps by the government were sporadic, they have now become constant and frequently have been combined with evacuation of whole villages and the establishment of permanent posts. These operations create obvious problems for the infrastructure apparatus. Some elements defect when the village is evacuated, but if cadres remain behind, they face rather uncertain prospects. They must survive through their own efforts without village support, sometimes hiding in the jungle. The function of survival may still be carried out, but under such circumstances the cadres serve little useful purpose in promoting the business of the Viet Cong movement. The effect on morale can be easily appreciated, though it should not be overestimated.

There is some debate over the question of where the Viet Cong apparatus in the countryside can be most critically and permanently damaged—at its head or at its feet. A vital element of the infrastructure is communication between the decision-makers and the lower-level executors who are merely tools. While the lower-level personnel may be less important in a hierarchical sense, they do the work of the organization, and in the remarkably inflexible Viet Cong organization, their weakest characteristic is their tendency to become paralyzed, at least temporarily, in the absence of direction from above. Therefore, it is sometimes argued that destruction of the district-level transmission link could prove the most effective means of destroying the village infrastructure. However, some observers state that the defection of a great number of "little brothers" can have an equally damaging effect, since policy-makers without tools can accomplish nothing.

While the increasing Viet Cong defection rate is impressive, caution should be exercised in the interpretation of this as a sign of general weakening of the infrastructure or a decline in morale. Few hard-core infrastructure cadres have rallied to the South Vietnamese Government side. The vast majority of the civilian returnees are farmers or low-level NLF members forced into serving the Viet Cong. These people support the side which exerts the stronger influence in the area at a given time. By the same token, while "search and destroy" operations do disturb the infrastructure apparatus, it must be recognized that this is only temporary. Unless military operations are closely followed with successful revolutionary development activities in an area by Saigon and its allies, the infrastructure tends to return to the area and assume control once again.

Viet Cong Leadership:
Shadowy and Featureless

One of the most striking differences between the Viet Cong movement and the earlier Communist revolutionary models lies in the nature of the ranking leadership. The Viet Cong have frequently been referred to as "faceless," an epithet which is not exaggerated. It is applicable to both public and clandestine leadership. In contrast to the great hero-figures who emerged from the Chinese revolutionary struggle and the Indochina War—Mao Tse-tung and his famous marshals and Ho Chi Minh with his eminent strategist Vo Nguyen Giap—no figure of remotely comparable stature has appeared in years of relatively successful Viet Cong guerrilla warfare in South Vietnam. Although Hanoi has selected some suitable non-Communist figures to form the Central Committee of the NLF and to head its numerous functional groups, these persons not only have no real power, but they are also largely unknown or obscure persons as far as the Vietnamese public is concerned. No prestigious figure in South Vietnam, no matter how strongly in opposition to the Saigon government, has gone into the jungle with the NFL. Prominent opposition personalities among the educated elite have either completely retired from public life or have expatriated themselves to the comforts of Hong Kong, Paris, or the United States.

On the overt level, the best the Communists could produce as a chairman for the National Liberation Front was a nondescript Saigon leftist lawyer named Nguyen Huu Tho, who, since the Front's founding, has carried on his decorative duties as head of the NLF Presidium in a manner apparently quite satisfactory to his masters. The somewhat more dynamic Secretary-General, Huynh Tan Phat, is said to be an architect by profession, and seems to make a more distinct impression on foreign visitors and newsmen.

There are 15 members of the Presidium of the NLF, of whom 12 are reputedly not Communist Party members. However, those 12 all have long histories of pro-Communist front activities and several may actually be Party members. There are six vice-presidents of the Presidium, and it is among these that the three known Communist Party members are found. Among the Presidium members are two Buddhist leaders (one a clergyman), a representative of the *Cao Dai* religious sect, and a *montagnard* of the Rhade tribe. No Presidium member is well-known in South Vietnam on the basis of an independent public reputation.

True anonymity, however, characterizes the real leaders of the Viet Cong. Identification of these men and the roles they play is a matter of some controversy among specialists, but there is general agreement on certain points. There is undoubtedly some member of the *Lao Dong* Politburo in Hanoi charged with special responsibility for the struggle in the South. Both Le Duan, the Party First Secretary, and Nguyen Chi Thanh have been mentioned as this over-all mentor, and perhaps both have been involved at one time or another. Attached to the *Lao Dong* Central Committee is a Central Reunification Department, which seems to be the link between the *Lao Dong* Politburo and the South, and which is headed by North Vietnamese Army General Nguyen Van Vinh. Over-all field direction in the South may be under a *Lao Dong* Central Committee member working under an alias. Operational headquarters in the South is the Central Office for South Vietnam, located with the NLF in Tay Ninh Province (or in Cambodia, depending on Allied military pressure). It is probably headed by Tran Nam Trung, member of the NLF Presidium and chairman of the NLF Military Committee. More significantly, he is Secretary-General of the People's Revolutionary Party, and he is also quite likely one and the same person as Lt. Gen. Tran Van Tra of the People's Army of North Vietnam (PAVN). It is also reported that the director of all Viet Cong activity in the northern third of the country is North Vietnamese Major General Nguyen Don.[48]

The difficulty in identifying the military high command is accentuated by Communist propaganda on the NLF armed forces. One of the fantasies perpetrated by Hanoi is the publicity build-up of Nguyen Thi Dinh, an obscure lady of gentle appearance, as the Deputy Commander in Chief of the NLF Armed Forces. Little background for this martial title is revealed in her biography as given by Hanoi, which reads as follows:

> Representative of the South Vietnamese women is Madame Nguyen Thi Dinh, a 45-year-old woman, native of Ben Tre. Together with her husband she had taken part in revolutionary activities in the 30's. Then her husband was exiled in Poulo-Condore island and died there, while she was imprisoned during 3 years. Hardly was she released than she participated in the 1945 August Revolution, then in the resistance war against the French colonialists. After peace was restored, she had to hide herself in bushes day and night to avoid savage terrorism conducted by the U.S.-Diem. But she was not disheartened by privations and hardships and succeeded in launching the armed uprising in Ben Tre, thus opening a new stage of struggle carried

---

[48] Further discussion of the Viet Cong leadership can be found in George Carver's "The Faceless Viet Cong" in *Foreign Affairs,* April 1966, and in Takashi Oka's "The Other Regime in South Vietnam" in *The New York Times Magazine* of July 31, 1966, p. 46. Pike, *op. cit.,* contains a detailed biographic appendix.

out both politically and militarily by the South Vietnamese people. Then she unceasingly contributed an important share to the cause of the South Vietnam National Front for Liberation which leads the resistance war against the U.S. imperialists and their henchmen with a view to liberating the South and advancing towards the reunification of the country.

At present Madame Nguyen Thi Dinh is at the same time chairman of the South Vietnam Liberation Women's Union, Presidium member of the Central Committee of the National Front for Liberation and deputy commander-in-chief of the South Vietnam liberation armed forces.[49]

Why this strange obscurity in the leadership of a movement to which so much is attributed—a movement which is looked upon by its adherents as the vanguard of the anti-imperialistic struggle, and which so many consider the culmination of the national revolution of the Vietnamese people? One possible answer comes fairly easily to mind. The peculiarly shadowy nature of the higher-level Viet Cong leadership is probably one indication of the tightness of control by North Vietnam, whose leaders may wish to make certain that no strong and attractive figure arises in the South who might at some time or another take an embarrassingly independent posture. There are reports that Hanoi may even be using the device of frequent rotation of political cadres and military leaders to prevent the development of independent power bases in South Vietnam.

Yet this extreme jealousy of control by an outside power poses a serious question of success or failure for a movement such as that of the Viet Cong. While all insurgencies need some degree of extramural support to win, unless the incumbent does absolutely nothing to prevent rebel success, they must also generate the kind of independent momentum which

---

[49] Intersol, Hanoi, *Solidarity with South Vietnam*, No. 9, August 1965, p. 11.

requires a persuasive program and attractive leaders to articulate policies and capture popular imagination. This requirement, however, may be less important in an insurgency whose roots are essentially exogenous. In such a case, organizational and operational techniques probably have priority over inspiring programs and leadership.

In fact, organization has been the key to NLF success. The builders of Viet Cong organization and the practitioners of its operational doctrine may well enjoy great prestige in the areas in which they work. However, this does not translate itself into the kind of magnetism that would be required to impress the populace of government-held or contested areas. Furthermore, whatever opportunity earlier and less pro-Hanoi leaders of the movement may have had for establishing a claim to national leadership was lost in the increasing tide of Northern cadres who came to direct the war. Their revolutionary prestige has been dissipated in the influx of professionals from the North who are far more interested in their careers than in Southern problems. The dominant father image of Ho Chi Minh has also helped to submerge potential Southern leadership.

Since the Viet Cong movement is now *in fact* more an imported product than a domestic one, leadership seems to be a lesser consideration; however, as the movement is being *promoted* as a native enterprise, the dynamics of its public posture would seem to require far more than the shapeless gray which characterizes its top echelon.

Viet Cong Operational Policies and Problems: The Mobilization of Popular Support

As previously stated, the NLF has drawn no significant support from the elite of South Vietnam. General popular support is another matter. Because of variations in Viet Cong tactics for mobilizing support, the unevenness of Saigon's response to these challenges, and the changing fortunes of war, this is an area in which it is very difficult to make valid assessments. We do know, of course, that the Viet Cong have staked their main hopes on control of the peasantry, who constitute some 80 per cent of the population, and in so doing they follow the Chinese and Viet Minh pattern. It is not certain to what extent they have been successful, since most estimates of percentages of the peasant population, pro-Viet Cong, pro-Saigon, or neutral, are of dubious value. However, the fact that all resistance to the Communists in the countryside did not collapse, even in the bleakest period militarily, indicates that the Viet Cong have had difficulty in winning over the peasantry, and particularly in getting their fullest material support.

Most available evidence points to almost continuous Viet Cong unhappiness over the "slack" and apathetic attitude of the peasants, and the leaders of the movement have been quick to sense the emptiness of much of the mass activity promoted by the NLF in the villages. Too often the peasant has been willing to accept the material benefits of Viet Cong policy (e.g., a piece of land) and then has lost interest in the larger goals of the Revolution. However, the NLF administration has found ways of overcoming traditional rural Vietnamese distrust of *all* government. One method has been to enmesh the peasant within his functional association in activity which is progressively more militant—donations to the insurgent movement, assistance in recruitment of young men into guerrilla ranks, construction of simple booby-traps or spiked boards for defense of the village, etc. Whenever possible, the Viet Cong recruit prominent local personalities as village "liberation" committee chairmen, with the expectation that these men will develop a group of loyal and devoted believers in the village.

Great attention and much publicity are given to security

needs and security measures, mostly for the purposes of popular mobilization. The peasants are endlessly warned against the "dangerous elements" in their midst and the "vile stratagems" of the enemy in the countryside. Intensive indoctrination efforts are launched to combat "counterrevolutionary tendencies" and to protect classified information. Recalcitrant "reactionary" persons are put under close surveillance, and considerable efforts are made to remold their thinking.

Recruitment is an area in which the Viet Cong work extremely hard to promote active participation by the villages in the "liberation" war. Giving a son to the guerrilla ranks has become a measure of great revolutionary devotion. The Viet Cong use family ties to great advantage for recruitment into the guerrilla units, for if one member of a family joins, others are likely to follow. There is also a hostage system of sorts; the recruit is sometimes sent some distance away for duty and serves as a hostage for his family's good performance in supplying the Viet Cong with food, money, shelter and information.[50]

Only when a village or hamlet has been cleansed of "enemy agents," has organized itself thoroughly into "liberation" associations and committees, has provided adequate physical security against the enemy, has organized "mutual-aid" teams, and has made arrangements for regularly providing the NLF with recruits, supplies and intelligence, can it be considered truly "liberated" and qualified for what the Viet Cong call a "combat" status. Viet Cong documents testify that the task of creating such an ideal structure has been very difficult. However, indefatigable pursuit of this goal without undue interference has been made possible for the Viet Cong in many areas because of the destruction of the government's presence and

[50] Pike, *op. cit.*, pp. 286-293.

the elimination of the natural village leaders who refuse co-operation with the NLF.

Viet Cong policies and problems in mobilizing support from the peasantry in South Vietnam are illustrated in a captured 1965 manual entitled "Rural Support Policy." Various aspects of agricultural taxation are discussed in this document, particularly the evasion of taxes by the peasants through devious ruses and the problems this causes the Viet Cong leadership:

> With their will to resist the enemy, with their great love for their country, our people contributed men, goods, talent and force to the Revolution in the past year. Financially, our people have sacrificed a great portion of their incomes to supply the needs of the Revolution . . .

> There were also a small few who fabricated ways to delay or reduce their contributions, sometimes deliberately to avoid paying at the end of the fiscal year. This has caused many problems for the public fund. Some people do this because they are ignorant and have not yet realized that the U.S. imperialists and their lackeys are carrying on a war of aggression and conquest to change South Vietnam into their colony and to make our people their slaves. Therefore, we, the people of the entire nation, must resist them in order to keep ourselves free. Hence, each citizen has a duty to contribute labor, forces, and wealth to the Revolution according to his ability, not according to his inclinations.

> Not fully realizing their duty to their country, some wish to contribute little and claim to have less land than they do. . . . They declare their land to be of poorer quality than it is; . . . Some did not pay fully, some have not yet paid, some have prolonged and delayed their payment period . . . Some even waited for the price of rice to rise so as to gain greater benefits from it.

> In order to increase the public fund this year, the farmers must contribute according to a policy that will assure that each citizen carries out his legal duty equally and

encourages him to increase his productivity to assist the people's forces. Hence, all must sacrifice part of their farming productivity as a contribution to the Revolution. They will, in doing this, guarantee the needs of the Revolution and life of the people. . . .

Paying fully and on time will permit public funds to be gathered to provide the Revolution with all of its needs as well as to give it a reserve fund whenever the Revolution's needs increase for expensive operations that will accomplish greater victories.

This will give the cadres more time to accomplish other tasks. . . .[51]

Political mobilization of the masses was certainly much easier for Mao Tse-tung and Ho Chi Minh in their earlier wars than it has been for the Viet Cong since 1958. In China and Indochina the direct physical assault of the Japanese and French armies brought about an unprecedented degree of nationalist feeling and social mobilization which the Communists skillfully exploited and developed. In South Vietnam, despite the massive efforts of Communist propaganda, there has been no imperialist aggressor, no colonial occupier, no foreign exploiter upon whom to focus popular hostility in a meaningful and credible way. Furthermore, whatever the failures and excesses of the Saigon governments—Ngo Dinh Diem's iron regime or his military successors—they have not been intolerable by Asian standards, and it is quite likely that in the absence of the armed insurgency, the country would have continued to prosper as it did for the first five years after the Geneva partition.

Some parts of the following captured Viet Cong directive may seem ludicrous. However, the substance represents a

---

[51] Translation by Research Institute on Communist Strategy and Propaganda, University of Southern California, 1966.

serious effort on the part of the Communists to achieve something more than merely passive acceptance by the innately conservative peasants in the Viet Cong areas. Promotion of the "glorious families" emulation movement in the countryside is an attempt to obtain the kind of enthusiastic popular participation in revolutionary activities achieved by the Chinese Communists in parts of north China after 1937 and by Ho Chi Minh in Tonkin during the war against the French—a fervency not very evident in South Vietnam:

> The "glorious family," propounded by the Party, is instrumental in strengthening the Revolution. To build "glorious families" is to turn those families in the liberated countryside into resistance families, fully dedicated to the cause of the Revolution for the country's salvation.
>
> The establishment of the "glorious family" has a three-fold purpose:
>
> To motivate the masses to do their bit for the patriotic war; that is, to contribute manpower and material resources to the war against U.S. imperialists and their henchmen; to bring to fruition the national democratic revolution and at the same time to increase production and save. . . .
>
> Paralleling the above mission, efforts are directed towards the institution of a new way of life among the country people. It is characterized by an economically, politically, culturally, and ideologically sound society, which will serve as a stepping stone to subsequent progress towards socialism. . . .
>
> Stress the role and capability of the women, particularly women laborers and farmers. . . . Conduct indoctrination on the significance of the movement and stage mass rallies; play up the typical achievements of some families for commendation. . . .
>
> Subsequent to the massive, enthusiastic indoctrination at the inception of the program, elaborate indoctrination and

propaganda efforts should be directed towards the infrastructure of the movement to instruct the masses how to
build up "glorious families." . . . Institute an elaborate
commendation and grading system to select the "glorious
families." . . . Commendation and awards are given in the
form of land grants, commendation certificates, honor flags,
etc. And "glorious families" enjoy the respect of the community.[52]

Another prime concern of the Viet Cong is the Army of the
Republic of Vietnam (ARVN). The Communists were well
aware of the fact that before American intervention this force
was the main physical obstacle to Viet Cong takeover of the
country and that prior to the U.S. combat commitment it was
the only real impediment to Viet Cong victory. Despite weak
anti-guerrilla doctrine, poor leadership, many reverses, and ap-
palling casualties and desertions, the ARVN has grown stronger
and generally fights well. Cracking this tough nut through
propaganda and subversive proselyting has always been a key
problem for the Viet Cong. As the rank and file of the ARVN
represent the populace as a whole, the results of the *binh van*
(military proselyting) strategy reflect to an appreciable extent
the success or failure of the Viet Cong in breaking down popular
will to resist.

The importance the Communists attach to undermining the
Armed Forces of the Republic of Vietnam (RVNAF, as they
are called by the Communists) is illustrated in a Viet Cong
document captured in August 1965, entitled "Policies of the
NFLSVN Toward Officers and Men Serving in the Republic of
Vietnam Armed Forces":

. . . The NFLSVN calls on all patriotic troops and
officers serving in RVNAF to save yourselves and your
country. Cooperate with the people to establish a united

---

[52] Translation by U.S. Military Assistance Command, Vietnam, November 1965.

farmers, workers and soldiers front to resist the American imperialists and their lackeys; . . .

The official policies of the NFLSVN towards RVNAF soldiers and officers are as follows:

(1) We protest the present conscription policies of the American imperialists and their lackeys in SVN.
(2) We protest all cruelty and ill-treatment directed toward troops.
(3) We protest American military advisement and direct control of RVNAF units.
(4) We call on all patriotic troops and officers serving in the RVNAF to return to their families. . . . Troops and officers who return to their families and the revolutionary ranks will enjoy freedom, and will be assisted in securing a living. . . . RVNAF personnel who participate in actions against Americans and their lackeys are particularly assisted if they suffer any consequences. . . .

Awards and high employment are reserved for RVNAF personnel who act against the Americans and their lackeys. Those who convert to the cause will benefit from the clemency policy, even though they have committed crimes while serving in the RVNAF.

RVNAF personnel who lay down their arms benefit from the clemency policy and their lives are respected. Injured personnel are cared for. Corpses absolutely are not violated. Those who are killed in action will be buried in accordance with national rites, if the situation allows.

We unite to assist the dependents of RVNAF personnel. The people unite to assist all honest dependents of RVNAF personnel. They are assisted in daily activities and enjoy land policies and all other privileges. Those dependents who play their part in the deactivation of RVNAF will be welcomed and cited by the people and the NFLSVN . . .[53]

---

[53] Translation by U.S. Military Assistance Command, Vietnam, 1965.

The urban populace has not been overlooked by the Viet Cong, despite the movement's principal reliance on the peasantry. There undoubtedly have been periods in which the Communists were quite hopeful that political upheavals in the cities and towns would give them a decisive advantage, but so far they have been unable to organize a following in the urban areas or seriously threaten the towns and cities, which remain firmly in government hands. Viet Cong efforts continue, however, as the following captured 1965 directive on urban propaganda will illustrate:

> To be really successful in conducting propaganda missions, it is necessary that machinery be set up to help party committee echelons guiding propaganda missions.
>
> All Party members, Liberation Association members and people who are sympathetic toward the revolution should be propagandists.
>
> The Liberation cells are propaganda cells having the mission of:
> (1) Verbally propagating the main substance of leaflets, papers, magazines, information bulletins, and disseminating the mission.
> (2) Distributing papers and magazines, information and leaflets.
> (3) Collecting news in the city which relates to the enemy's crime, oppression and robbery.
> (4) Recording public opinion.
>
> In addition to the propaganda cell, it is necessary to organize the people working in collective places who can disseminate news and create public opinion in a prompt manner. For instance, in each market, a propaganda cell should be selected among . . . middle-aged female agents to propagandize victories and spread our influence.
>
> In hairdressers' shops, barber shops, and bicycle repairmen's shops, agents should be placed to assume this duty.

In each classroom and each [business] enterprise, a propaganda cell should be available and placed under the guidance of the school or enterprise party chapter.

In the city, the main propaganda vehicle is by mouth. Papers, magazines, and leaflets are to be disseminated only among Party members and the agent network.

To have a wide influence, propaganda should be transmitted from mouth to mouth among the population.[54]

Another element of South Vietnamese society which the NLF must take into consideration in policy-making is the highland minority. These tribal peoples—ethnically, linguistically, and culturally entirely different from the lowland Vietnamese—occupy a strategic position on the central plateau where the infiltration trails from Laos enter South Vietnam and where many of the Main Force units of the Viet Cong and the North Vietnamese Army are concentrated. Largely because of the ineptitude Saigon has frequently shown in handling these more primitive people, the Communists have made serious headway among the *montagnards*. However, this progress would undoubtedly have been more decisive if the Viet Cong had not committed some of their most brutal terroristic acts against certain tribal villages.

A Viet Cong directive captured in 1966 explains the ostensible NLF policy toward ethnic minorities:

Though their numbers are small, our fellow citizens in the ethnic minorities occupy a large and important strategic area. . . .

The Revolution takes *montagnard* problems seriously . . . Our leadership must guide the minorities to save themselves and their country. The watchwords are unification, democracy, autonomy and mutual aid. . . .

---

[54] Translation by U.S. Military Assistance Command, Vietnam, November 1965.

The policy of the NLF is as follows:

(1) Ethnic minority peoples are the brothers of all Vietnamese . . .

(2) We shall create conditions for the ultimate achievement of regional self-government of the tribal peoples after the liberation of the country.

(3) In the new democratic government, the minority peoples will have the vote and will elect their candidates for both local governments and the National Assembly.

(4) Mutual self-help among the minority peoples is encouraged.

(5) The minorities will have freedom to develop their own culture, religion and mores, and to use their own languages.

(6) The ethnic minorities have a right to bear arms in self-defense.

(7) We must increase cooperation and mutual relationships between the various tribal groups.

(8) Our minorities must learn that their main enemies are U.S. imperialism and its stooges.

(9) We must narrow and then eliminate prejudices among minority groups and among these groups and the ethnic Vietnamese.

(10) The eventual autonomy of the regional governments will be local, subject to higher echelons of government in matters of common policy.

(11) Every cadre and revolutionary soldier must recognize his responsibility for seeing to the feeding, clothing, schooling, health and enthusiasm of the minority peoples.

(12) We must help the minority peoples to improve their living conditions by stabilizing and developing the economies of their areas.

(13) Equality between men and women must be established.

(14) Strong inducements to desert must be given ethnic minority soldiers in the enemy ranks.[55]

While this policy has little meaning in practice, it does sound good to some of the tribal minorities, who have long been the victims of discrimination, and a number have been subverted by the Viet Cong.

Not all Viet Cong material support is extracted from the peasants. Entrepreneurs, both large and small, have been forced in many instances to pay taxes and tribute to the Viet Cong in order to survive, particularly if they are vulnerable to personal intimidation, have fixed property subject to Communist attack, or transport goods to market through insecure areas.

The following is an example of a 1965 Viet Cong leaflet intended for distribution to Saigon businessmen for fund-raising purposes. Although the element of extortion is overlaid with the language of patriotic exhortation, the threat is nonetheless evident:

NATIONAL FRONT FOR LIBERATION
OF SOUTH VIETNAM

> Independence-Democracy-
> Peace-Neutrality

SAIGON-GIA DINH REGION
#887

> TO: _____

The national liberation revolution of the people against aggression to gain independence, democracy, peace and neutrality will surely be successful.
Various classes of people in rural areas and cities, especially the farmers, workers and laboring class, are contributing

---

[55] Translation by Research Institute on Communist Strategy and Propaganda, University of Southern California, June 1966.

large amounts of money and are sacrificing much bone and blood in the struggle for the liberation of the Fatherland. As saving the country is the common mission of everybody, the contribution of money to the Revolution is also a mission of every patriot.

We appeal to you, in the interest of the Fatherland, to contribute your part to the Revolution.

Such an act will symbolize your patriotism, and *guarantee your legal privileges at present and in the future.*

Our greeting for victory

FOR NATIONAL FRONT FOR LIBERATION OF SVN SAIGON-GIA DINH REGION

Deputy Chairman

Engineer Le Van Tha

(Signed & Sealed)[56]

Terror: A Key Operational Weapon

Intimidation and coercion have been the stock-in-trade of the Viet Cong. Force has been necessary to overcome an apathetic popular response to the Communist program. A strongly motivated civilian population, which is the traditional source of recruitment and support for guerrilla bands, did not exist in South Vietnam when the insurgency began. The interests of the South Vietnamese peasant center almost entirely on his family, rice field and village, while larger political matters concern him very little. Although he would naturally like to improve his living standard, he has not tortured his soul with yearning for unification of the "Fatherland." However, the

---

[56] Translation by U.S. Military Assistance Command, Vietnam. November 1965. Italics added.

Viet Cong have proved one point in this war: a guerrilla move-ment does not need an actively friendly population in order to thrive. It can do very well with a passive one which owes little loyalty either to incumbent or insurgent. It can overcome this inertia and gain support by a combination of persistent persua-sion, brutal coercion, military success, and a demonstration of an absolutely ruthless determination to win. These are the ele-ments by which the Viet Cong grip on the countryside is main-tained.

One of the key elements of the Viet Cong's combination of operational techniques is the strategy of terrorism. The Viet Cong have used terror to great effect ever since the beginning of the war, and they have widened its scope along with direct military attacks. The intensity of this use of terrorism as an operational weapon is unprecedented in Asian Communist experience and may well be the Viet Cong's unique contribu-tion to the art of revolutionary war.

Of course, terror was present in earlier Communist move-ments. It was used by the Chinese Communists during the agrarian uprisings in the 1920's and during the period they were in Kiangsi in the early 1930's, but once Mao gained complete control of the Party, terror was soft-pedalled for a time, and emphasis was placed on the subversive persuasion of both offi-cials and the people. Mao apparently understood the counter-productive potential in prolonged large-scale terrorism during the civil war operations, where the emphasis instead was on winning friends and influencing people. Accordingly, for the most part, he waited until after the consolidation of state control by the Party before unleashing the grim purges of the land-reform program.

Similarly, Ho Chi Minh reserved the full fury of the terror until after his government had been established in Hanoi. During the conflict with the French, Ho mercilessly purged the non-Communist political leaders who refused to cooperate with him and dealt harshly with certain pro-French towns and villages, but he never felt the need at that time for the kind of widespread terrorism in the countryside which the Viet Cong practice unceasingly today. Instead, like Mao, he waited for the 1954-1956 land reform movement to launch the blood bath in North Vietnam, which, some experts estimate, claimed over 100,000 victims. In addition to present Viet Cong atrocities, the memory of that period is still a major factor in the unwillingness of most South Vietnamese to be unduly impressed by Ho's program and propaganda today, or to be enthusiastic about the prospects of life under Communism.

Viet Cong "agitational terror" in government-held or contested areas takes several forms: (1) acts which accompany assaults on hamlets, military installations, or armed forces units; (2) harassment fire on villages for coercive purposes; (3) acts of terror committed in connection with frequent Viet Cong ambushes; (4) direct violence through sabotage; and (5) acts directed against specific individuals, such as kidnapping, assassination, torture, and execution. Bombings and grenade-throwing in the cities and towns are the most spectacular form in terms of publicity; the incessant nerve-wracking harrassment of villages is perhaps the most pervasive type. However, terror directed against individuals probably has the most serious immediate effect and portends the gravest long-range threat to a stable South Vietnamese society.

Some general rules for the Viet Cong's campaign of personal terror throughout South Vietnam were given in a directive captured in the "D" Zone in January 1966 and written about a month earlier:

> The plan for elimination of tyrants [i.e., assassinations] must be very carefully worked out. Investigation of those to be eliminated must be meticulously conducted. Leaflets

must be disseminated to make the people clearly understand the crimes of the tyrants to be executed and our
motives in executing them and to warn other tyrants.
The plan for the elimination of tyrants must be very
detailed so that our personnel can withdraw safely after
accomplishing their mission. Men must be deployed to prevent enemy pursuit, if any, and leaflets disseminated . . .

Then take advantage of the deaths of tyrants to terrorize
the enemy generally and cause the lowest echelons of his
organization to disintegrate . . .[57]

Another part of the same document referred to the need for
terrorist attacks on Americans and high Vietnamese officials in
the cities:

During the month . . . [we] attacked policemen who
were searching people in the streets [of Saigon] and also
attacked police stations. The Directorate General of
National Police headquarters was attacked by our Liberation Army. These attacks caused confusion in the enemy
ranks and aroused enthusiasm among the people . . .

. . . Enemy officials dare not oppose us. Policemen dare
not stay in slums at night. Those guarding remote areas
[of the city] are withdrawn . . . Policemen enter the slums
now only in groups . . .

Targets: in addition to attacks launched against personnel in the enemy's lowest echelons we must deal heavy
blows against high ranking enemy personnel. Only blows
like the attack on the Directorate General of National
Police headquarters and on Americans can have the proper
repercussions, hurt enemy prestige and exert sufficient pressure on the low echelon personnel. Therefore our attacks
must be essentially aimed at wicked enemy ringleaders
. . .[58]

---

[57] U.S. Mission in Vietnam, *Viet Cong Use of Terror: A Study.* May 1966, p. 23.
[58] *Ibid.*, pp. 21-22.

Despite the intended target discrimination, the victims of these attacks are mostly ordinary Vietnamese civilians. The common citizen came under stepped-up Viet Cong terroristic pressure in the period preceding the elections for a Vietnamese Constituent Assembly in September 1966 and during the village elections in the spring of 1967. Anxious to disrupt these elections, the Viet Cong increased their efforts in both countryside and city. Despite this campaign, the populace turned out in record numbers to vote, thereby casting considerable doubt on the effectiveness of Viet Cong terror in influencing specific critical issues.

It should be remembered, however, that the insurgents have never exercised their real terror capabilities for achieving short-term objectives; they have preferred to pursue a long-range relentless campaign in the countryside. In July 1964, Australian Communist newsman Wilfred Burchett quoted a Viet Cong official regarding a typical assassination campaign:

> In each village . . . We compiled a detailed dossier of the various local despots. If someone merited the death penalty we sent a group to deal with him. Afterwards we used loudhailers to explain the crimes committed . . . we posted names of other tyrants who would be dealt with if they did not cease their activities . . . The executions . . . and the warnings . . . played a major role in breaking the grip of the enemy throughout the country . . . and created conditions under which we could move back into the villages, either permanently or in organizational visits . . .[59]

The Viet Cong use terror for two basic purposes. It is designed to break down Saigon's authority and the established social order by elimination of opposing forces and by disorientation and isolation of the individual Vietnamese through fear,

---

[59] *Ibid.,* p. 24.

anxiety, and despair. Terror is also calculated to boost insurgent prestige by morale-building within the rebel ranks and by publicizing the movement among the populace. Although it was not a factor in earlier years, the Viet Cong may also have recently used terror as a means of compulsory recruitment in the countryside.

Breakdown of the governmental structure and social order is the central objective of the rebels, and this purpose is most effectively served by acts of terror against individuals. Viet Cong use of murder and torture has been deliberate and systematic, not, to their way of thinking, purely wanton or sadistic. Both in doctrine and practice, such terror is considered by the Viet Cong to be properly used when it is calculated for maximum effect, applied judiciously and selectively, and alternated with persuasion as local circumstances dictate. Nevertheless, the scale of the effort is appallingly impressive. It is estimated that some 16,000 officials have been assassinated since 1957 and that approximately 10,000 have been kidnapped. Studies indicate that a much larger number of non-official natural village leaders have been victims, as well as uncounted numbers of ordinary civilians. Any and all representatives of Saigon's authority in the countryside—not only village chiefs, but schoolteachers, aid officials, medical teams, road crews—are fair game for this campaign of murder, kidnapping, and intimidation. In contested areas there is evidence that the Viet Cong select as targets the ablest and most popular officials, as well as the least capable and most detested members of the civil service. The result, obviously, is mediocrity in public administration.

Some authorities conclude that the Viet Cong have wiped out almost the entire class of native village leaders who have been recognized in their communities because of age, experience, wisdom, or integrity. This virtual genocide will have the deepest and most serious long-range effects on efforts to bring order and stability to South Vietnam, even if the Viet Cong lose militarily.

It is amply evident that in this "struggle for men's minds" the ground rules for the Viet Cong are a remorseless application of Mao Tse-tung's famous credo: "Political power grows out of the barrel of a gun." Their systematically applied terror has been undeniably effective, but it may be yielding diminishing returns. There has to be a certain random quality in terror; some of its effectiveness would be lost in complete predictability. However, there is evidence that in the last year it has become indiscriminate to the point of being counterproductive. This violence may indeed have become a disease, a compulsive addiction which overrides any doctrinal restraints. At least, there is no question but that the Viet Cong are carrying on large-scale terror campaigns long after such activities theoretically would have become only marginally effective. However, the absence of physical security in the countryside, even in areas where the Viet Cong have been bested in battle, allows the terrorists more latitude for profitable operation than the theoretical "norm."

Viet Cong Propaganda Efforts: Massive and Sustained

While the Viet Cong use physical violence and persuasive personal contact as their main weapons, they carry on a massive campaign of printed and broadcast propaganda. The NLF has an elaborate news and propaganda arm which operates several clandestine "liberation" radio stations within Viet Cong-controlled areas and publishes veritable mountains of "liberation" news sheets, broadsides, and "slogan slips." Some of these are printed under the government's nose in Saigon and the provincial towns, others in crude shops in the jungle or marshlands. However, much of the more elaborate propaganda work is done in Hanoi, especially the publication of material for foreign consumption. Of course, North Vietnam's regular government and Party media provide outlets for a great amount of material on the NLF and Viet Cong.

The propaganda effort directed toward the masses is carried on by thousands of *agit-prop* cadres in the villages and in clandestine urban cells, who not only prepare the written material but also frequently address meetings. Viet Cong media output indicates that the Communist propagandist in South Vietnam, at least until recently, has generally played down Marxist ideology (which he probably doesn't understand very well, anyway) and has concentrated on exploitation of special grievances of specific groups. Ironically, while the social turmoil arising from decades of violence in Vietnam is the main asset of the Viet Cong, the peasant understands little or nothing of social issues; therefore, the *agit-prop* cadre must appeal to him in a direct, harsh, and unsophisticated manner.[60]

Most important among the vehicles for the promotion of ideas are the social organizations sponsored by the Viet Cong— the farmers', women's, youth and cultural associations. These groups develop a sense of community which intensifies the impact of ideas and information and give the average Vietnamese the feeling, as he participates in the process, that his efforts have an effective social meaning. Such groups have been extremely useful to the Viet Cong in generating discontent, aggravating hatreds and mobilizing these passions for promotion of NLF objectives. The peasant succumbs more easily to fallacious argument and emotional appeal in such organizations, because his capacity for critical judgment is lowered in the

---

[60] Joint U.S. Public Affairs Office, Saigon, "Review of Current Viet Cong Propaganda Efforts." JUSPAO Field Memorandum No. 2, September 30, 1965.

milieu of the group. *Agit-prop* activities within the various associations are designed to change the peasant's entire outlook toward his world and the government and to channel his attitudes in directions chosen by the Viet Cong.

The primary theme of *agit-prop* activities is hate. An NLF Central Committee directive states, "To guide the masses toward the Revolution, the *agit-prop* arm must make the masses hate the enemy. . . . Promotion of hatred must be permanent, continuous. . . ."[61] A secondary theme is idealism, the concept of building a new and better society through the revolution. Finally, there is the crucial appeal to material self-interest, such as the promise of land. If this last theme were the only requirement for complete success of the Viet Cong propaganda effort, the task would be relatively easy, for this is the one appeal to which the villager has responded. The great and difficult problem of the Viet Cong propaganda is to lift the peasant beyond the concept of self-interest into full participation in advancing the revolution's goals.

If the statistical evidence provided by captured Viet Cong propaganda material is a reasonably reliable guide, the principal target among the special groups is the South Vietnamese Army, which, despite its weaknesses, has been one of the groups most difficult to influence. An annual catalog of 500 Viet Cong documents collected by the U.S. Information Service shows that by far the largest number targeted to a specific group (96) were directed at the ARVN. The second most prominent target (28) was youth, and the appeal in many of the documents addressed to young people was centered on avoiding military conscription.[62] More recent Viet Cong media output continues to

---

[61] Pike, *op. cit.*, p. 284. Chapter 7 of this work is an excellent study of Viet Cong communication processes.

[62] U.S. Information Service, Saigon, Special Programs Division, February 1, 1963.

emphasize the critical importance of military proselyting through propaganda.

A call to ARVN units to surrender and join the Viet Cong is featured in this propaganda brochure of late 1964, acquired in the autumn of 1965:

> LETTER TO OFFICERS AND NON-COMMIS-
> SIONED OFFICERS IN POSITIONS
> ENCIRCLED BY OUR FORCES
>
> It is high time for you to wait no longer. Before the tempestuous rising wave of the revolution of the South Vietnamese people, the American imperialists and their lackeys are suffering serious military and political losses. . . .
>
> . . . we are tightening our encirclement and are determined to liberate this area by annihilating your unit.
>
> Being an officer who is more or less concerned with current events, you may be clear-sighted enough to evaluate the situation and to take proper and reasonable action.
>
> We suggest two following actions to you:
>
> (1) All your unit cooperate with us to fight the Americans. Tyrants who resist you should be annihilated immediately. The National Liberation Front will ensure your interests and positions and will properly praise your achievements.
> (2) When the guns are sounding in battle, listen for the megaphone call to surrender and order your soldiers to surrender. Annihilate those who resist you. You will be praised and actively helped.
>
> We hope that upon receipt of this letter, you will immediately reach a decision; the sooner the better. . . .[63]

Although ARVN performance in battle has been uneven, and a few units have surrendered when heavily pressed, there

---

[63] Translation by U.S. Military Assistance Command, Vietnam, November 1965.

is no direct evidence linking these incidents to the efforts of Viet Cong propaganda. Bad morale arising from poor leadership has usually been the cause.

The ARVN was the target of the following blandishments in a leaflet of late 1964:

OFFICERS AND SOLDIERS IN THE SOUTHERN ARMY—

While you live through these horrible times under guerrilla fire from troops of the Liberation Army, while your corpses are piled up high as a mountain, while your blood flows like a river, do you know that:

In Saigon, a group of generals—lackeys of the Americans—are still not satisfied with their fabulous luxuries. While you are dying, they are jostling each other for higher positions in the government, cutting each other into pieces in order to obtain the best positions of power for themselves. . . .

Each of them strives to be the first running-dog of the American aggressors. . . .

Comrades: The U.S. imperialists and their henchmen have duped you, have taken advantage of your sacrifices on the battlefield to lengthen the tenure of their own rotten and corrupt regime.

Would you voluntarily die to defend the selfish interests of these shameless people? You should think this over carefully . . .

Thousands of soldiers in the South are continuously deserting their army and thousands of other soldiers have rebelled or come back with their weapons to join the revolutionary movement.[64]

---

[64] Translation by Research Institute on Communist Strategy and Propaganda, University of Southern California, November 1965.

The last paragraph of the above leaflet is unfortunately partially true. Thousands of ARVN personnel have deserted, posing a problem which continues to vex both the South Vietnamese and American commands. However, most of these deserters are new draftees who leave for a variety of personal reasons, usually returning to their families, and then frequently coming back to their military units. There is no evidence they join the Viet Cong in any numbers. As far as the higher officer echelons are concerned, it is significant that the NLF, unlike the Chinese Communists, has been singularly unsuccessful in enticing government military officers to defect and bring their units into Viet Cong ranks.

The Vietnamese soldier may at times be callous and brutal, but the Viet Cong attempt to exploit any latent distaste for bloodletting he may have. An appeal to conscience, with overtures to personal identity, is featured in this 1963 broadside at the South Vietnamese military:

LET US NOT KILL, BURN AND ROB THE PEOPLE! "SWEEP AND CLEAR" MISSIONS ARE TO KILL THE PEOPLE.

SOLDIERS, OFFICERS IN THE ARMY OF THE SOUTH:

Helicopter "sweep and clear" operations push you into killing and wounding many comrades, the majority of whom are children, women and the aged. . . . Among the people killed by these operations have been dozens of families of soldiers, officers and public servants—families like that of Lt. Thanh [security officer of Soc Trang] of Phy My Village. His mother was wounded, his nephew was killed and his father's altar was smashed, while the incense burner was thrown out into the yard. Another family suffering losses was that of Mr. Van at the Song Doc market. He was shot to death during these operations while fishing. Mr. Van has two uncles who are government officers . . .

Soldiers and officers:

Those mentioned above who were killed, do you know who they are? Are they not your own parents, your own wives, your own brothers, members of your own family and of your own race?

Let us resolve not to kill, burn and rob the people! [65]

Of course the peasant is a prime target for Viet Cong propaganda. Material directed at him has frequently emphasized appeals for economic support of the NLF and for sabotage of the government's population and resources control in the countryside. In an earlier period the government's program centered around the "strategic hamlet" plan in which whole groups of peasants were moved into special "secure" hamlets built by the government. The program was criticized in both concept and execution by American and other observers, and it quickly became a prime and vulnerable target of the Viet Cong propaganda machine.

A 1961 general appeal to the peasant population to resist the "strategic hamlet" plan of President Diem is couched in these terms:

A recent propaganda drive by the U.S.-Diem clique has announced the advent of the Strategic Hamlet program, by which Vietnamese will allegedly live together in peace, harmony and security. . . .

What is this U.S.-Diem monstrosity called "strategic hamlets"? It is a jail, a giant concentration camp surrounded by barbed wire and earthen walls. Day and night U.S.-Diem soldiers will be strictly guarding it. Many of our unfortunate fellow citizens will be forced to live in these hamlets like birds in a cage or like fish in a net.

---

[65] Translation by Research Institute on Communist Strategy and Propaganda, University of Southern California, November 1965.

> Our comrades will be forced to live under strict regulations and oppressive orders They will be used as shields against the bullets aimed at U.S.-Diem forces. You, brothers and comrades, will be the soldiers who carry U.S.-made rifles to kill your own comrades. Women will be raped or will become the playthings of American military officers. . . .

> Can this plot be carried out? One thousand times No! The "strategic hamlet" plan cannot fool anyone. Its true face is unmasked! . . .

> We must oppose the building of these hamlets. We must continue struggling to destroy the entire plan of occupation by the American invaders! [66]

More recent propaganda aimed at the peasants has reflected the Viet Cong's urgent need for more rice, money, supplies and recruits. In late 1965 important themes included appeals to farmers not to relocate as refugees in government areas and not to bring grain to central government storage areas for safe-keeping.

Viet Cong propaganda efforts in the cities have been persistent but largely unproductive. Most of the appeals for uprisings, strikes, and demonstrations have failed, and the Communists have had to content themselves with only marginally effective infiltration and exploitation of the other political movements which dominate the populous centers.

An example of the generally unrewarded efforts of the National Liberation Front to obtain support in the urban areas is the following portion of a so-called "Summons of the Labor Liberation Front in Saigon-Gia Dinh for Labor Day, May 1, 1965":

> Workers and comrades in Saigon-Gia Dinh! . . .
> . . . to save our people from foreign slavery, to liberate

---

[66] Translation by Research Institute on Communist Strategy and Propaganda, University of Southern California, November 1965.

our comrade workers from oppression and to celebrate May 1, the Labor Liberation Front calls upon comrade workers to:

(1) Unite and join the liberation movement, to ask for essential rights, to oppose mobilization, to demand peace, to cease aggressive war and to ask for a U.S. withdrawal.

(2) Emphasize all tricks played by Americans and their lackeys. The only way to establish peace and true independence is to chase U.S. imperialists out and to overthrow the treacherous government.

(3) The united strength of worker comrades is unbeatable. . . . The unity of workers and peasants is invincible in the struggle against the U.S. aggressors.

Bravely stand up, all comrade workers!
May 1 spirit forever! [67]

The crudest and most ineffective Viet Cong propaganda is directed at the American serviceman in Vietnam. There is no reason to believe the Communists expend any great effort in this direction, but a number of printed pieces in "English" have been picked up since mid-1965. The low potential of some of these efforts can be gauged from the examples on pages 131 and 132.

In addition to their massive effort within South Vietnam, the Viet Cong mount an extensive propaganda campaign abroad, designed to promote support for the revolutionary cause in Vietnam and to undermine sympathy for Saigon, as well as to "isolate" the United States. In fact, since the overseas representatives of the NLF are not recognized as full diplomatic representatives of a government, their duties are primarily propagandistic.

A very detailed document concerning foreign propaganda

---

[67] Translation by Research Institute on Communist Strategy and Propaganda, University of Southern California, November 1965.

U.S Armymen in South VietNam !

Dying for the defence of the fatherland is an honour for an armymen !

But dying when serving a war of aggression is not only a loss for your family, but a loss a shameul end.

Full respéct to the 1954 Génvea Agreemént on VietNam !

VietNamese Internal Affairs must bé settled by the VietNamese People Themselves !

To Black American service men in the South Viet-nam.

— On August 14, 1965 seven thousand American Negroes in Los Angeles were doWn in the street protesting against racial discrimination and against the dirty War made by the U.S. Imperialists in Viet-nam. The negro demonstrators shouted out as they went :

« wE DON'TwANT TO GO IN FIGHT IN VIFT-NAM ! WE WANT ₁O FIGHT FOR OURSELVES RIGHT HERE ! »

— Are you decided to sacrifice your life for the interest of the U.S. capitalists Who are perseeuting your families and race ?

— join your countrymen in demanding your immediate repatriation.

— The Viet-namese and Black American people have but one common enemy : the U.S. imperialists.

— Down with U.S. imperialism !

— The U.S. imperialists must stop the dirty war in South Viet-nam and their brutality against the Black American people.

The South Viet·nam National Frent for Liberation.

YOUR happinessis not to be found in the battle from! it's in your sweet home beside your parents, wife and children.

By opposing the U.S. impercalists aggressive war in south Việt-nam, you prattically defend the noble ideals of American people's year 1.863 revolution.

140.000 troops lost their lives in Korea! don't tel such an ordial reoccured! Tens of thousands of American mothers wines want into mourning for their dear men fallen in Korea, don't let such a plight reccu through the south Việt-nam.

The french 250.000 strong expeditionary corps was routed our here! don't follow in their foots-teps.

efforts was captured by U.S. Army units on March 10, 1967 in Operation Junction City in Tay Ninh Province. Written in June 1966, it provides an analysis of successes and failures of earlier efforts and projects future missions. Apparently prepared at the request of Hanoi, it makes very clear that North Vietnam directs and controls external propaganda. The report states, "The bulk of the propaganda and diplomatic activities is assumed by North Vietnam" and goes on to say that "major problems are settled by the Party Central Committee and the Front's Party Group, under the guidance of the Central Office for South Vietnam . . ." Among the tasks assigned to the NLF external communications effort by this directive are the following:

> Keep abreast of the American people's opinions and try to motivate youths, intellectuals and religious sects to protest the war of aggression waged by their government. . . . Motivate families of U.S. troops dispatched to Vietnam to protest . . .

> Wisely arouse acute internal dissension among the imperialist countries—chiefly between France and the USA— to win the support of France and her [followers] . . .

> Make sweeping efforts to enlist sympathy and support from the Afro-Asian and Latin American countries . . .

> At present, the deep dissension between Russia and China . . . [has] ruined the consistency of action of the pro-Vietnamese Socialistic bloc . . . Make sweeping efforts to enlist support and aid from the Socialist countries, especially the Chinese and Russians . . .

The Viet Cong Fighter:
Tough, Patient, Skillful

In the ranks as well as the leadership, the Viet Cong combine qualities both similar and dissimilar to those of the men in earlier Communist guerrilla movements. The Viet Cong fighting man in the first-line units (i.e., those bearing the brunt of military actions) has never been the kind of lightly armed civilian the guerrilla is traditionally thought to be. In fact, the word "guerrilla" is almost a misnomer in his case. He is a thoroughly trained and rigidly indoctrinated soldier who has been amply supplied with both the tactical skills and weapons he needs for the kind of fluid war he fights. Whereas the Chinese Communist and Viet Minh guerrilla fighter had his war thrust upon him by his opponent and learned as he went along, the Viet Cong soldier has had his struggle meticulously planned for him. Like his earlier counterparts, he is daring, resourceful, ruthless, a skillful improvisor, and, above all, tough and patient. However, he is often very young, and since he lacks individual initiative, he looks to his officers and political cadres as the source of all wisdom and guidance. Therefore his morale tends to be brittle and it seems to have been shaken considerably since 1965 by the aerial attacks and ground offensives of the American, South Vietnamese, and Allied forces.

It has been said that guerrilla warfare is an art form and that the Viet Cong are not just craftsmen but true artists. They have indeed perfected the traditional guerrilla tactics of mobility, surprise, and concealment. They have a superb intelligence network which usually gives them an advantage either in battle or in avoidance of battle (avoiding battle frequently being a critical matter with guerrilla forces). In their careful planning of ambushes and surprise attacks, they frequently rehearse for days or weeks with crude practice models set up in jungle clearings. As Mao Tse-tung so explicitly advised, the Viet Cong generally attack only when they can concentrate swiftly and enjoy locally favorable odds; they refuse a fight or break it off if the situation turns against them. Sometimes, however, they fail to observe this principle and are badly mauled. The most important recent development is that U.S. and South Vietnamese military power has increasingly deprived them of their long-enjoyed ability to choose the place, time, and manner of engagement.

Viet Cong Morale under Stress: A Key to Peace in Vietnam?

The question often arises: Can the Viet Cong be defeated? Perhaps it should be more accurately phrased: Will the Viet Cong ever realize they are militarily beaten? Despite the setbacks suffered in the last two years, the NLF continues to sound a public note of stubborn and confident defiance.

On the fifth anniversary of the NLF, the Chairman, Nguyen Huu Tho, restated the Viet Cong's determination to continue fighting:

> The just militant stand of our people and the Front is a consistent one. No schemes or methods, however sinister and cunning, no force on earth, however brutal, can make us depart from the road we have chosen or force us to sell off our sacred national rights. So long as the U.S. imperialists have not put an end to their aggressive war, withdrawn all U.S. and satellite troops and weapons from South Vietnam, and let the South Vietnamese people settle their own affairs, our whole people will continue to hold their guns firmly and fight resolutely to the end. Even if we have to fight for another 10 or 20 years, or longer, even if we have to fight through this and the next generation, we shall not hesitate for a moment. Having a solid political and military basis and firmly grasping the factors for victory, our whole people and army will resolutely march forward to win final victory. Our people will certainly be completely victorious.[68]

---

[68] *Vietnam News Agency*, Hanoi, December 21, 1965.

Nine months later, with loss of Communist military initiative evident on all fronts, Mr. Tho again avowed Viet Cong willingness and ability to fight on against all odds. In an interview with leftist Australian newsman Wilfred Burchett, Tho was somewhat defensive, however, and indicated a slight retreat from his previous position that the NLF program would have to be accepted in advance of peace negotiations:

> The Americans have the most powerful military and economic potentials in the Western world, but we have the invincible power of the people's war . . . Politically and morally we are absolutely stronger than the Americans. . . .
>
> We are ready to fight to the end . . . until the territories inherited from our ancestors are liberated from the U.S. aggressor's yoke. . . .
>
> . . . the Vietnamese people are eager for peace. . . . But peace must be achieved on the basis of independence and democracy. . . . Therefore, the conditions for a genuine peace . . . and for a correct solution to the South Vietnam problem can only be:
>
> (1) The Americans must end the aggressive war . . . and withdraw . . .
> (2) The Americans must respect the rights of the South Vietnamese people. . . .
> (3) The NFLSV, the only legal representative of South Vietnam, must be present at and have a decisive voice in any political solution in South Vietnam. . . .[69]

Despite the brave talk, it is known that Viet Cong morale has been sagging for the last year. The Communists have not only been denied victory; they have been remorselessly attacked by allied forces. While some captured Viet Cong continue to show defiance, many others make it very clear they are seriously

---

[69] Liberation Radio (clandestine), South Vietnam, September 13, 1966.

perturbed. Defections have steadily increased, doubling in the spring of 1967 over the previous period. Some evidence of the erosion of morale in the face of the reversal of military fortunes can be seen in the following excerpt from an editorial in the theoretical journal of the People's Revolutionary Party in January 1966:

> Practically speaking, this situation has created much difficulty for the political struggle movement and has caused a number of comrades who are not thoroughly imbued with the policy and strategy of the party to be confused about the role of the political struggle . . . and about the efficacy of the political struggle in view of the increasing number of U.S. expeditionary troops in South Vietnam. . . . In a number of regions, the party leadership spirit appears to be less versatile and creative. . . .[70]

Exhortations to the cadres to overcome bad morale appeared in a document captured in March 1966:

FROM: FRONT PARTY COMMITTEE

TO: PARTY COMMITTEE MEMBERS

Dear Friends,

In order to heighten the morale of our men and to increase our victories in the future, the Front Party Committee has decided to suspend our operations temporarily in order to reorient and revamp training assignments . . .

Our suspended period is rather short, but it is an important period during which we must prepare our offensive positions for future battles. . . . You must understand the importance of our mission and the value of this period of history in order to put forth a great effort to determine the outcome.

---

[70] *Tien Phong*, January 1966.

TO ACHIEVE THIS MISSION YOU MUST:

(1) Unite the party committee members from the regiment down to the chapter committees; unite all cadres, soldiers, and members. Everyone must constantly overcome hardships and difficulties in all actions. You must realize that the time to regroup, reorient, and increase morale is not the time to relax. You must realize that night is not to be used for wasting time and doing nothing. Some people have the appearance of working while they are actually relaxing.

(2) Help the cadres retain their qualities and abilities in tactics, technology, organization and command.

(3) In the training period as in the organization period it is necessary to prepare specific plans and measures in detail.

(4) . . . Try to overcome difficulties by mutual support and spirit. Attempt to unify the soldiers and try to improve their morale. The cadres must set good examples for the soldiers.[71]

By the late summer of 1966, the situation had apparently become sufficiently serious for the Viet Cong to call a special conference of all the political officers of the military units to discuss the difficult problems of maintaining morale in the face of adversity. The importance of such discussions cannot be overemphasized, since Asian Communist armies are above all political organizations, and erosion of the psycho-political structure can bring rapid deterioration. A commentary on this conference in an NLF military paper had this to say about the problems of morale in general and of retrenching to lower-level protracted guerrilla warfare in particular:

> . . . The political task demands that great attention be given to conducting steady and continuous training on the revolutionary situation and tasks; to developing to a high

---

[71] Translation by U.S. Field Force, Vietnam, March 1966.

degree of revolutionary heroism; and to building the spirit of fighting a protracted war, of relying mainly on one's strength, of conducting continuous attacks, of scoring repeated victories, and, at the same time, of combating and overcoming all subjective phenomena such as stopping halfway, not clearly distinguishing between the enemy and us, nurturing illusions about peace, and fearing what needs a long time to be accomplished and is full of hardships.

The political task must shed light on the logic of the people's war and our unique military art, develop the ability of man and of the masses in order to defeat an enemy much stronger than we in the material field, force him to fight on our terms, and subdue his spirit of aggression with our "determination to fight and win" spirit . . .

It is necessary to improve the cadres in all aspects . . . . . . In the building of the Liberation Armed Forces, the role of the political task—the soul of a revolutionary armed force—must not be neglected . . .[72]

One object of particular concern to the Viet Cong leaders is Saigon's psychological warfare programs, especially the *chieu hoi* or "Open Arms" campaign, which has led to increasing defections from NLF ranks (13,500 from January to May 1967). A Viet Cong district commander's directive of December 20, 1966 admitted that "the impact of increased enemy military operations and the *chieu hoi* programs has, on the whole, resulted in lowering the morale of some ideologically backward men, who often listen to enemy broadcasts, keep . . . enemy leaflets, and wait to be issued their weapons in order to go over to the enemy side." Another directive from a Viet Cong provincial committee, captured in the "Iron Triangle" north of Saigon on April 2, 1967, indicated to what extent this "ideological back-

---

[72] *Quan Giai Phong* (NLF Armed Forces Paper), September 18, 1966.

wardness" had penetrated some areas, and it then went on to prescribe countermeasures:

> . . . defense against psychological warfare and "open arms" was not rigorously undertaken. As a result, many soldiers and workers have lost spirit and become demoralized. . . . Some of our soldiers and cadres . . . have surrendered. . . ., carrying important documents and weapons with them. . . . As compared with 1965, the rate of desertion is higher. In some areas the number of soldiers and cadres who deserted or defected . . . as a result of appeals of their families amounted to 80%. . . . Some defectors . . . have shown the enemy our base areas and installations, thus causing much damage. . . .

> . . . Security protection . . . against the enemy's psywar . . . constitutes the most important and urgent mission. . . . Increase the work of . . . ideological education to raise the level of revolutionary consciousness. . . . Pay special care to the improvement of material life for those . . . who are in difficulties. . . . Grasp fast the people who have doubtful political tendencies. . . . The core elements . . . should be pure and clean. . . . Special emphasis should be placed on the education of the soldiers' families in weak areas. . . .

The Viet Cong have attempted to boost flagging morale by concerted output of exhortative commentary in published and broadcast media. Central to this effort has been the theme that any successful moves of the Americans and the "puppet" Saigon government represent only the desperate lunges and thrashings of a "grievously wounded wild beast." While the documentary evidence indicates field commanders in the South do not grossly underestimate their own losses when reporting to Hanoi, fantastic inflation of figures on American and South Vietnamese casualties is the rule. Military developments have not been the only occasions for such distorted comment. Even so serious a political setback as the complete failure of the Viet Cong to disrupt the September 1966 Constituent Assembly elections was the subject of much self-deluding propaganda output. Despite this, however, the acceptance of hard "protracted struggle" rather than early victory is very apparent in the following Viet Cong radio broadcast:

> One is not surprised when the U.S.-Thieu-Ky clique publishes huge figures on the number of voters and the high percentage of voters going to the polls in order to propagandize their imaginary success. The Americans, Thieu, and Ky are regular liars and they have lied in a not very clever manner . . .
>
> For the absolute majority of our people—that is, some 10 million people who have been liberated—this Constituent Assembly is meaningless. In this South Vietnamese territory, the only genuine organization which has the right to represent our people and is actually representing them is the NFLSV, which is organizing and leading our people in conducting the national salvation resistance . . .
>
> For the people in the areas under the temporary control of the enemy, this "Constituent Assembly" does not have any authority. It reflects only the U.S.-Thieu-Ky clique's determination to counter the will of our people. Through their indifference, boycott, and open opposition, our people have clearly manifested their stand, which is not to recognize the assembly molded by the U.S.-Thieu-Ky clique. . . .
>
> The anti-U.S. national salvation resistance of our people is developing strongly. Our people and army have achieved repeated victories on all battlefields.
>
> The enemy is going downhill, while our people are winning. Our good opportunity is even clearer. Our people are determined to move forward urgently to win brilliant successes along their path of protracted resistance war.[73]

---

[73] Liberation Radio, South Vietnam (clandestine), September 12, 1966.

That the Communists in South Vietnam have lost their chance for military victory seems indisputable. If they were in fact on the verge of moving into the offensive Phase III of "people's war" in early 1965 when U.S. forces intervened, that plan was completely aborted and the opportunity is unlikely to recur. While the insurgents are far from defeated militarily, they have won no significant victories since 1965, and their prestige, as well as their own morale, seems to have waned.

The decisive development in this period has been the Allied denial to the Viet Cong of their most cherished military asset —the initiative, the ability to choose the place, time, and manner of their attacks. With the aid of regular North Vietnamese troops, they may yet launch an offensive of desperation, or they may on the other hand decide to "de-escalate" their posture to purely hit-and-run guerrilla attacks by very small units, in the hope of wearing down American patience. (The Chinese have apparently been urging the latter course.) However, either course would be fraught with extreme danger. The first would expose the Communist main forces to possible annihilation. A fall-back to lower-level war might well discredit the movement and create critical morale problems. As Gen. Giap himself has said, unless a guerrilla movement advances steadily from success to greater success and evolves into some kind of regular warfare, it cannot win a decision; instead, it is likely to stagnate and wither, as happened in Malaya and the Philippines.

Documents captured in 1967, containing confidential speeches and commentaries by the North Vietnamese military leaders who direct the war, seem to reflect this concern that a slowing down would be dangerous. In one such memorandum, Gen. Nguyen Chi Thanh puts it this way: "On the principle of waging a long-range struggle, tremendous efforts are to be made to obtain decisive victory within a relatively short period of time."

On non-military levels, however, Viet Cong chances are brighter. Terror is still a very useful tool, if not so effective as before. The Communist political apparatus remains intact and permeates the countryside, particularly in the critical Mekong Delta area. Until more permanent physical security is provided by Allied forces and the Saigon government in areas where the Viet Cong have been militarily routed, the enemy will continue to infiltrate and re-establish control. However, there is evidence that attitudes of the peasant toward the Viet Cong have become more hostile in the last year, and where a minimum of security is provided, there are signs that his behavior may be changing in the direction of more cooperation with Allied forces. In addition to a pronounced dearth of battle victories, two factors work against the Viet Cong. First, without adducing moralistic considerations which may have little bearing in a land steeped in 25 years of bloodshed and cruelty, the Viet Cong's apparent need to continue their massive terror seems to call into question the whole psycho-political foundation of their appeal to the Vietnamese people. Second, the significance of the fact that this highly touted "indigenous" insurgency had to be reinforced by the North Vietnamese Army troops *before* American combat forces arrived is unlikely to have escaped the notice of the South Vietnamese.

There might be such a collapse of organization and spirit that the Viet Cong would be unable to continue even politically. It appears, however, that the Viet Cong's best opportunity for the future would lie in a reversion from the "armed" struggle to the "political" struggle, *provided* morale of the cadres can be sustained in the process. The Vietnamese Communists did this twice before—at Geneva in 1954 and in Laos in 1962—and they may do so again, if they should decide that this would be the most advantageous course for them. When Ho Chi Minh and other *Lao Dong* leaders speak of a 20-year struggle, they do not refer exclusively to the military phase. To them struggle includes all aspects—political, psychological, economic, and social. Which element to stress at any given time depends on the circumstances of the moment and the future prospects. The view of negotiations which Hanoi applies to the war in the South is summed by in a speech to Viet Cong cadres by Gen. Nguyen Van Vinh, Chief of the *Lao Dong* Reunification Department, text of which was captured in the spring of 1967:

> At present, the situation is not ripe for negotiations. Fighting while negotiating is aimed at opening another front. . . . Our policy is to continue fighting until a certain time when we can fight and negotiate at the same time. . . . Thus we will take advantage of the opportunity offered by the negotiations to step up further our military attacks [and] political struggle. . . .

This North Vietnamese general also makes it plain that the NLF will have little to say about peace negotiations: "The Party Central Committee entrusts the Politburo with the task of deciding on the time for negotiations."

Nevertheless, with or without formal negotiations, a reversion to political struggle in South Vietnam may take place. There is no reason to believe that the vast political and subversive apparatus of the Viet Cong will ever be voluntarily dismantled. Even if military action ceases, its potential for interference with the orderly development of free South Vietnam will be high. Only an effective long-range rejuvenation of the South Vietnamese body politic can neutralize it.

Whatever the future political problems, if it is demonstrated that the Viet Cong cannot win this phase of the struggle by force of arms, a significant round will have been won against the challenge of Communist revolutionary warfare. Then the serious social, political and economic problems of South Vietnam can be tackled in an atmosphere of reasonable physical security which is indispensable to progress.

V

The Chinese Posture: Aggression with Caution

Vietnam is clearly one of the "wars of national liberation" which Peking hopefully projects for the "colonial areas" of Southeast Asia and elsewhere. In view of Communist China's increasing militancy, Peking's position and attitudes on Vietnam take on an added significance. The issue is all the more important in the light of Communist China's recent emergence as a nuclear power—even though, at the moment, Peking is scarcely in the same class as the charter members of the club.

Neither the ancient history of the Empire nor the record of Communist Chinese behavior in recent times is reassuring with respect to Vietnam. For nearly a thousand years the Chinese occupied what is now the northern part of Vietnam, and in the centuries following Vietnamese independence they made several more attempts at conquest. The Chinese Emperor traditionally exercised suzerainty over Vietnam and strongly opposed French occupation in the 19th Century. China has assisted revolutionary movements in Vietnam since the beginning of this century, and it is to be suspected that these efforts have not been altruistic. There is some disagreement among scholars over the extent to which the Chinese Communists exercised decisive influence over the Viet Minh movement after they reached the Indochina border in 1949, but to this day the tone of Peking

pronouncements on Vietnam has been unmistakably propri-
etary. Within our lifetime, Chinese Communist military forces
have been committed outside of China's traditional borders: in
Korea, in Tibet, and in India. Moreover, Communist China
has been providing substantial material aid to North Vietnam.
This aid has taken the form of weapons, supplies, food, and
technical assistance. Peking has provided Hanoi with both technical personnel and engineering units as well as some railway
labor battalions. Most of the arms now used by the Viet Cong
are of Chinese origin. Careful analysis of Chinese Communist
military policy over the past two decades, however, shows it to
have been one of pursuing aggressive aims with caution. The
top Peking military command has rarely been reckless. Mao
and Company consistently talk loudly, but clearly carry a little
stick.

Although the war in South Vietnam began as Hanoi's design,
without need or evidence of Chinese instigation, the Peking
Communists have increasingly come to see it as an invaluable
vehicle for the promotion of their designs in Southeast Asia
and for the substantiation of Maoist doctrines of "people's war."
It has come to mean for them a crucial arena in which U.S.
forces can be dispersed and worn down, and as a struggle which,
if successful, will decisively increase Peking's ability to influence
the foreign and domestic policies of the Southeast Asian states.
This vested interest in the Vietnam War has grown year by
year, so that while China has remained very cautious about
actual intervention in the struggle, Peking has become the
fiercest opponent of a peaceful solution.

Despite Communist China's caution, it would be well not
to ignore completely the pronouncements from Peking, especially as the military establishment of Defense Minister Lin
Piao looms larger in the Peking policy planning picture and as

the so-called "Proletarian Cultural Revolution" throughout mainland China proceeds on its fateful way.

Repeatedly, Peking has issued warnings to the United States on Vietnam. The majority of objective observers do not take these warnings seriously: that is, they do not regard them as ultimatums. However, these statements have their obvious place in the Peking propagandists' design, and they certainly have their impact within and outside of China.

The Chinese Communist Commitment in Vietnam: Bellicose but Vague

Immediately after the Tonkin Gulf incident in August 1964, the Government of the Chinese People's Republic issued a harsh statement of denunciation and warning:

> On August 5, U.S. naval aircraft made a surprise attack on the Democratic Republic of Viet Nam, successively bombing the areas of Nghe An, Hon Gay and Thanh Hoa. Thus U.S. imperialism went over the "brink of war" and made the first step in extending the war in Indo-China. The situation is of the utmost gravity. The Government of the Democratic Republic of Viet Nam has lodged a strong protest with the U.S. Government. The Chinese Government fully supports the just stand of the Democratic Republic of Viet Nam.

> The Government of the People's Republic of China hereby solemnly declares: The flames of a war of aggression against the Democratic Republic of Viet Nam were lit by the United States. Since the United States has acted this way, the Democratic Republic of Viet Nam has gained the right of action to fight against aggression, and all the countries upholding the Geneva agreements have gained the right of action to assist the Democratic Republic of Viet Nam in its fight against aggression. The Democratic Republic of Viet Nam is a member of the socialist camp, and

no socialist country can sit idly by while it is being subjected to aggression. The Democratic Republic of Viet
Nam and China are neighbours closely related to each
other like the lips and the teeth, and the Vietnamese
people are intimate brothers of the Chinese people. Aggression by the United States against the Democratic
Republic of Viet Nam means aggression against China.
The Chinese people will absolutely not sit idly by without
lending a helping hand. The debt of blood incurred by
the United States to the Vietnamese people must be repaid.
The U.S. Government must immediately stop its armed
provocations against the Democratic Republic of Viet Nam
and its armed encroachments on the latter's sacred territory, airspace and territorial waters. Otherwise, the U.S.
Government must be held responsible for all the grave
consequences arising therefrom.[74]

On April 2, 1965, after the commitment of American air and
ground forces in full combat, Chinese Communist Foreign
Minister Chen Yi made the following pledge to his North
Vietnamese counterpart, Xuan Thuy:

. . . The entire Chinese people are deeply angered at
the way U.S. imperialism rudely tramples the Geneva
agreements underfoot and recklessly commits aggression
against Viet Nam. We strongly condemn the piratical
behaviour of the Johnson Administration. . . . To help
the fraternal Vietnamese people resist U.S. aggression is
the Chineses people's sacred internationalist duty. We
firmly support the March 22 statement of the South Viet
Nam National Front for Liberation. The Chinese people
will exert every effort to send the heroic South Vietnamese
people the necessary material aid, including arms and all
other war materiel, and stand ready to dispatch their men
to fight shoulder to shoulder with the South Vietnamese
people whenever the latter so require. No matter what
U.S. imperialism may do next, the Chinese people will

[74] *Peking Review*, No. 32, August 7, 1964, pp. ii and iii.

unswervingly stand by the entire Vietnamese people and carry through to the end the struggle to defeat the unspeakably vicious U.S. aggressors.[75]

The Standing Committee of the National People's Congress of China (a rubber-stamp parliament), went so far as to mention preparation for the commitment of Chinese manpower to the Vietnam war, in a message to the National Assembly in Hanoi in the spring of 1965. This was the highwater mark of bellicosity and specific commitment in Chinese statements on the Viet Nam war:

> The Standing Committee of the National People's Congress calls on the people's organizations and the people throughout the country: . . .
>
> —to study conscientiously the relevant statements issued by our Government and the relevant editorials of *Jen Min Jih Pao,* to carry out education on patriotism and internationalism and, together with the people throughout the world, to launch a mighty mass movement to compel the U.S. aggressors to get out of Viet Nam;
>
> —to heighten vigilance, strengthen national defence, take an active part in labour, increase production, study hard and work hard, and by actual deeds assist the Vietnamese people in their just and patriotic struggle of resistance to U.S. aggression;
>
> —to make full preparations to send our own people to fight together with the Vietnamese people and drive out the U.S. aggressors in the event the U.S. imperialism continues to escalate its war of aggression and the Vietnamese people need them. . . .[76]

In the course of time, however, the Peking leaders began to hedge their promises. An illustration of a gradually lowering

---

[75] *Peking Review,* No. 14, April 2, 1965, pp. 10-11.

[76] *Peking Review,* No. 17, April 23, 1965, p. 7.

Chinese posture in regard to the Vietnam war commitment
came in Premier Chou En-lai's message on the fifth anniversary
of the founding of the National Front for the Liberation of
South Vietnam, December 1965:

> As a fraternal neighbour closely linked with the Vietnam-
> ese people like the lips and teeth, the Chinese Government
> and the 650 million Chinese people firmly support the Viet-
> namese people in their just struggle against U.S. aggression
> and for national salvation, and firmly support the four-
> point proposition of the Democratic Republic of Viet Nam
> and the five-part statement of the South Viet Nam National
> Front for Liberation. The Chinese people have long been
> prepared. Should U.S. imperialism insist on going further
> along the road of war expansion and having another trial
> of strength with the Chinese people, the Chinese people
> will resolutely take up the challenge and fight to the end.
> Come what may, the Chinese people will unswervingly
> side with the fraternal Vietnamese people and contribute
> all our efforts to the defeat of U.S. imperialism until final
> victory.[77]

It can be seen that this statement rather deftly changed the
emphasis from specific assistance for the hard-pressed Vietnamese to a warning against a direct American challenge to Communist China.

By February 1966, President Liu Shao-chi was even more
vague on the subject of assistance, as illustrated in his reply to
Ho Chi Minh's circular letter to the heads of Communist states:

> . . . It is clear that so long as the United States does not
> give up its aim of seizing southern Vietnam for itself, it will
> only be playing tricks to hoodwink people and using differ-
> ent means to achieve this aim, no matter how many points
> it may put forward and what stuff it may put into its
> "basket of peace."

---

[77] *Peking Review*, No. 52, December 24, 1965, p. 6.

If the Vietnam question is to be settled, the United States must truly abide by the Geneva agreements. The four-point stand for a settlement of the Vietnam question set forth by the Government of the Democratic Republic of Vietnam is a concentrated expression of the essence of the Geneva agreements. . . .

Respected and Dear Comrade President! The great struggle of the Vietnamese people against U.S. aggression and for national salvation is perfectly just. Your heroic deeds have inspired all revolutionary peoples, and your struggle has won the extensive sympathy and support of the peace-loving countries and people of the whole world. . . . China and Vietnam are neighbours closely related like the lips and the teeth; our two peoples are brothers sharing weal and woe. The Chinese people always unswervingly stand together with the Vietnamese people and wholeheartedly support and assist them in their just struggle. To whatever extent U.S. imperialism may expand its war and whatever may be the price we have to pay, we 650 million Chinese people will stand by the fraternal Vietnamese people in a joint struggle to thoroughly defeat the U.S. aggressors.[78]

A month later, Liu Shao-chi made it even more apparent that China was ready to fight the war to the last Vietnamese:

. . . The United States persists in its reckless course, and the Vietnamese people are determined, as they have long since declared, to fight on until the U.S. aggressors are thoroughly defeated.

. . . The heroic struggle of the Vietnamese people is a powerful support to the anti-imperialist revolutionary struggles of the people of Asia, Africa and the whole world. All Afro-Asian countries have the duty to support and help the Vietnamese people, and must not take a middle position between the aggressor and the victim of aggression.

---

[78] *Peking Review*, No. 6, February 4, 1966, pp. 5-6.

Together with the other Afro-Asian peoples, the Chinese people are determined to carry the struggle through to the end in supporting and aiding the Vietnamese people's fight against U.S. aggression and for national salvation, and stopping the U.S. imperialist aggression.[79]

The "lips and teeth" and "brothers sharing weal and woe" approach has continued to decorate Peking's statements of support to the Vietnamese Communists, but the only significant Chinese commitment has been an adamant opposition to a negotiated peace. In the development of this hard line, earlier Chinese support for a return to the 1954 Geneva Agreement has been abandoned.

After the U.S. bombing of the Hanoi-Haiphong oil complexes in July 1966, Peking seemingly felt compelled to restate its support of the Vietnamese Communists in stronger terms. A *People's Daily* editorial of July 18 reflected a renewed militancy without making precise commitments as to Communist China's course:

The Johnson Administration's bombing of Hanoi and Haiphong is a sign of its hopelessness after its endless defeats in the war of aggression against Vietnam. It vainly hopes to force the Vietnamese people to their knees and accede to its "peace talks" swindle by wildly escalating the war. . . .

The Chinese people's stand to firmly support the Vietnamese people to carry their struggle to resist U.S. aggression and save their country through to the end is firm and unchangeable. Our 700 million people are behind the Vietnamese people. The vast expanse of our country is the rear area of the Vietnamese people. We have already said what we wanted to say on this matter and we mean what we say. The U.S. imperialists further broke the bounds of war by their aggressive acts of bombing Hanoi and Haiphong,

---

[79] *Peking Review*, No. 10, March 4, 1966, p. 5.

and this gives us the right to further remove any restriction in aiding our Vietnamese brothers. . . . Whatever the risk or cost, we are determined to stand by the fraternal Vietnamese people and the revolutionary people of the world and give resolute support to the just struggle of the Vietnamese people until the U.S. aggressors are completely defeated. . . .

Final victory must belong to the heroic Vietnamese people![80]

Fantasy and Realism in Peking's View of the World Situation

Peking has shared with Hanoi a grossly distorted view of the importance of opposition in the United States and some other Free World areas to American policy in Vietnam. However, Mao's spokesmen have injected a much greater element of fantasy in their analyses. Chinese pronouncements view this dissidence not simply as a political embarrassment which will increasingly hamstring Washington in carrying out its Vietnam policies, but as a great revolutionary upsurge which will radically change the structure of American society and government.

A typical Chinese commentary on dissidence in the United States can be found in a *People's Daily* editorial on February 7, 1966, by "Commentator," a term usually applied to a person very high in inner Party circles:

The broad masses of American people underwent a profound revolutionary change when they rose up for the first time in history to fight the imperialists of their own country. . . .

---

[80] *Peking Review,* No. 30, July 22, 1966, pp. 18-19.

The popular demonstrations in many U.S. cities on 5 February, . . . highlighted the American people's spirited protest against and censure of the resumption of the bombings of North Vietnam and escalation of the war of aggression against Vietnam by the Lyndon Johnson administration. . . .

. . . The sweeping and unparalleled movement of the American people against this war of aggression in the past year hit hard at U.S. imperialism's policy of aggression and war. It came from that bulwark of capitalism like peals ringing out in a long, somber night to tell the world that the American people are in the process of a new awakening.

The Americans are a great people. In the past they had more than once stood up against imperialist wars of aggression. . . .

. . . The Lyndon Johnson administration's escalation of the criminal war of aggression against Vietnam drives the American people to a new awakening. Stern reality has opened their eyes and made them understand that this dirty war can only bring them endless misery.

The class conflict in the United States will inevitably become more acute. In their practice in class struggle, the American people will undoubtedly raise their political consciousness and organizational level. A greater upheaval may take place in American society. And many more new things will appear on the horizon of the North American continent. The American people's stormy struggle against the imperialists at home will inevitably rise to a higher level.[81]

On the other hand, Peking is not totally unaware of the fact that its clumsy diplomacy has succeeded in alienating most other nations. Communist China has from time to time moved from

---

[81] Peking Radio, February 7, 1966.

fantasy toward reality in viewing its position in a world which has not rushed to embrace Maoist doctrine.

One example of Peking's increasingly realistic assessment of the adverse trend of events in Vietnam, Southeast Asia and the world in general can be found in a *People's Daily* editorial of March 1, 1966:

> The present great upheavals on the international horizon are an inevitable result of the sharpening of class struggle and a salient characteristic of the international situation today. Upheavals are not a bad thing, but an excellent thing for revolutionaries. . . .
>
> In the eyes of revolutionaries, great upheavals are inevitable. They are a good thing, not a bad thing. . . .
>
> . . . The present era is one in which capitalism is heading toward extinction and socialism toward victory.
>
> The enemy is of course not reconciled to his defeat. The imperialists and reactionaries invariably use the most brutal means to suppress the revolutionary movements of the people of various countries. Even after the people have won victory in their struggles, they launch counterattacks and try in a thousand and one ways to restore their reactionary rule. Thus, victory in struggle is frequently intermingled with reverses and advance in movements with retreat. Under certain circumstances, a counterattack mounted by the imperialists and reactionaries may gain the upper hand for the time being, but this will only raise still higher the political consciousness of the people and mobilize still greater numbers, thereby helping the revolutionary movement to grow in depth and in scope on its onward march. Facts have proved and will continue to prove that no force on earth can impede or check the revolutionary movement of the oppressed peoples and nations, which will continue to leap forward despite the twists and turns in the road of advance. . . .[82]

---

[82] Peking Radio, March 1, 1966.

The recognition of ebb and flow in the fortunes of Communism was admitted again March 9, 1966 in *People's Daily:*

> They [Americans] may get the upper hand of the people in some places for some time as a result of their counterattacks. The movement of the people . . . seems to be on the ebb, but in reality, a new upsurge is brewing underneath. . . .

A tone of near self-pity crept into another comment from the same paper regarding deteriorating relations with Cuban Prime Minister Castro. General disappointment with events in Asia can be inferred:

> . . . Prime Minister Castro has gone very far down the road of opposition to China. People will wait and see how much further he will go. The Communist Party of China and the Chinese people are accustomed to being abused. Leaving aside the past, at present we are being abused abroad by the imperialists led by the United States, by reactionary nationalists, by the reactionaries of all countries and by the modern revisionists, and at home by Chiang Kai-shek, by landlords, rich peasants and counterrevolutionaries, bad elements and rightists. This has long been the case, and we are accustomed to it. Our attitude is: let them go on abusing us if they like; we will reply as and when necessary.[83]

Vietnam and the Rift with the USSR

Contrary to the predictions of some observers, the Vietnam War, far from healing the Sino-Soviet rift, has greatly exacerbated it. In fact, it has become the focal point of the quarrel. The increasing intensity of the Moscow-Peking disaffection is reflected in Communist China's constant use of Vietnam as an issue in its polemics against the USSR.

---

[83] *Peoples' Daily,* February 22, 1966.

Before looking at some of the specific documentation relative to Vietnam, it is essential to comment briefly on the basic nature and extent of Moscow-Peking disaffection. There is no doubt that the rift between the two Communist giants is very real.

Relations between the Soviet Union and Communist China began to deteriorate conspicuously in the late 1950's—after almost a decade of public, mutual admiration in the press of both countries. By the early 1960's the signs of separation, if not divorce, were unmistakable: The ideological dispute over such issues as "the path to socialism," "the virtue of the commune system," and "peaceful coexistence with the capitalist world" had begun to boil and was aired openly. It was at this time that Moscow unceremoniously withdrew its 13,000 Soviet economic and technical advisers from China and cut off further long-term credit.

The dispute then reached the stage of personal invective; Khrushchev branded Mao "a man old, but not wise, who reminds one of a worn-out galosh which can only be put in a corner of a room to be admired." Mao called Khrushchev a "Bible-reading and psalm-singing buffoon [and] a laughing stock."

Significantly, Peking charged Moscow with dragging its feet in military support to China and with refusing to assist China adequately in the development of nuclear weapons. Peking even asked Moscow for "sample atom bombs" but was refused.

Moscow, for its part, accused Peking of thousands of territorial violations of the Soviet border and with "interfering in the internal affairs of Communist parties throughout the world." This latter issue is especially galling to Moscow, which has for 40 years, in effect, controlled the Communist parties in most of the nations of the world. But the most astonishing exchange came over Africa, when a Chinese Communist delega-

tion asked the African leaders to follow Peking's rather than
Moscow's guidance, because, the Chinese said, "we, like you, are
part of the colored races." Responding to this and to the border
incursions, Moscow replied cuttingly in an official editorial, "we
hope we are not witnessing a return of the 'Yellow Peril'."

This, then, is part of the highly emotional backdrop for the
specific disagreement between Moscow and Peking with respect
to the situation in Vietnam.

Much of China's rage is undoubtedly caused by the increasing influence and leverage the USSR has obtained between 1965
and 1967 in North Vietnam through the supply of Societ missiles, radar and jet aircraft critical to Hanoi's defense against
United States bombing. Peking probably felt confident until
that time that the North Vietnamese Communists were safely
under its dominant influence. Now the Chinese leaders perhaps
see the increasing possibility of a settlement of the Vietnam issue
evolving under the influence of Soviet "revisionist" diplomacy
rather than Maoist revolutionary doctrine.

Lin Piao's classic article on "people's war," which was discussed earlier, contained a slashing attack on the USSR and on
its "revisionist" doctrine of "national-liberation war." Vietnam
was obviously what he had in mind:

> . . . The fundamental reason why the Khrushchev revi-
> sionists are opposed to people's war is that they have no
> faith in the masses and are afraid of U.S. imperialism,
> of war and of revolution. They submit to the nuclear
> blackmail of the U.S. imperialists and are afraid that, if
> the oppressed peoples and nations rise up to fight people's
> wars or the people of socialist countries repulse U.S. im-
> perialist aggression, U.S. imperialism will be incensed,
> they themselves will become involved and their fond dream
> of Soviet-U.S. cooperation to dominate the world will be
> spoiled.

We know that war brings destruction, sacrifice and suffering on the people. The sacrifice of a small number of people in revolutionary wars is repaid by security for whole nations, whole countries and even the whole of mankind; temporary suffering is repaid by lasting or even perpetual peace and happiness. War can temper the people and push history forward. In this sense, war is a great school. . . .

In the last analysis, whether one dares to wage a tit-for-tat struggle against armed aggression and suppression by the imperialists and their lackeys, whether one dares to fight a people's war against them, is tantamount to whether one dares to embark on revolution. This is the most effective touchstone for distinguishing genuine from fake revolutionaries and Marxist-Leninists. . . .[84]

One of the harshest notes struck by Peking in the quarrel with Moscow has concerned Soviet claims that China obstructed shipment of war material from the USSR to North Vietnam. An example of this was a story put out by the Chinese in January 1966:

It has been learnt from competent sources that Chinese Vice-Foreign Minister Wang Ping-nan received Soviet Ambassador S. G. Lapin in Peking on January 4. He handed the Ambassador a Chinese Government memorandum to the Soviet Government concerning the fact that the Soviet side has time and again spread rumours that China hindered the transit of arms to Vietnam.

The memorandum pointed out that the Chinese Government had always met the reasonable requests of the Soviet Government and had provided all possible facilities and assistance in the transport of arms in transit which were required by the Vietnamese side and which the Soviet side agreed to supply. Nevertheless, the Soviet side fabricated all sorts of rumours alleging that China obstructed the transport of Soviet military aid supplies to Vietnam and

---

[84] *Peking Review*, No. 36, September 3, 1965.

even asserting that China demanded from the Soviet Union payments in U.S. dollars for the transit of these supplies. . . .

The Chinese Government demanded in all seriousness that the Soviet Government take on itself the responsibility to clear up the rumours publicly, guarantee that similar incidents will not occur in the future, and give a reply at the earliest possible date. . . .

The competent Chinese sources pointed out that since February 25, 1965, when the Soviet side made its first request to China, the Chinese Government has met all the requests made by the Soviet Government and confirmed by the Government of the Democratic Republic of Vietnam for the transport of military aid supplies and technical personnel in transit to Vietnam. The Chinese railways without exception transported these supplies and personnel by special express military consignments. Every time Soviet supplies and personnel were brought to the Chinese border station, the Chinese side at once assigned waggons for their transport from the Sino-Soviet frontier to the Sino-Vietnamese frontier, generally not exceeding 10 days. The Chinese railways did this free of charge, receiving not a single kopeck, let alone one U.S. cent from the Soviet side. . . .

In addition to rejecting the Chinese Government's reasonable demand that the Soviet Government publicly clear up these rumours and guarantee not to manufacture them any more, Ambassador Lapin went so far as to unjustifiably refuse to accept the memorandum of the Chinese Government. . . .

. . . This practice on the part of the Soviet side cannot but be regarded as a new step along the road of worsening state relations between China and the Soviet Union. . . .

. . . Obviously, it has its ulterior motives in endlessly doing this. To put it bluntly, its purpose is to vilify China, sow discord in the relations between China and Vietnam and serve U.S. imperialism. . . .[85]

In April of 1967, reports began to circulate from countries with good diplomatic contacts in Communist capitals, that the Soviet Union and Communist China had worked out an understanding regarding the shipment of Soviet military equipment and supplies across Communist China. Such an agreement, if indeed it exists, is not very likely to redress the many years of bitterness and disagreement between Moscow and Peking over so many fundamental questions, of which Vietnam is merely symptomatic.

Perhaps the strongest recent theme in the Chinese diatribe against Moscow has been the charge that the USSR is collaborating with the United States in Vietnam and elsewhere, as in this editorial in *Red Flag*, the Chinese Communist Party's theoretical journal:

> Soviet-U.S. collaboration has been further stepped up on the question of Vietnam. While the United States was making a "pause in the bombing" and raising a hue and cry about "peace talks," [Aleksandr] Shelepin took pains to visit Hanoi in close coordination with this U.S. "peace talks" plot. The new leaders of the CPSU have also reached a tacit understanding with the United States on the European situation, so that the United States can transfer more and more troops from Europe to expand the war in Vietnam. The new leaders of the CPSU have uttered some words of support for Vietnam and given her some aid, but their aim in all this is to get more of a say for themselves on the Vietnam question, sow dissension in Sino-Vietnamese relations and help the United States to realize its "peace talks" plot. In the final analysis, they want to find a way out for U.S. imperialism on the Vietnam question, enable

---

[85] *Peking Review*, No. 4, January 21, 1966, pp. 26-27.

it to occupy South Vietnam permanently and strike a political deal with it. . . .[86]

Then came Peking's rejection of Moscow's invitation to attend the 23rd Congress of the CPSU in March 1966, in which Vietnam is again made an issue:

Dear comrades:

. . . Since Khrushchev's downfall, we have advised the new leaders of the party on a number of occasions to make a fresh start. We have done everything we could, but you have not shown the slightest repentance. . . .

Since coming to power the new leaders of the Soviet Communist party have gone farther and farther down the road of revisionism, splittism and great power chauvinism. . . .

Despite the tricks you have been playing to deceive people, you are pursuing U.S.-Soviet collaboration for the domination of the world with your whole heart and soul.

Your clamor for "united action" especially on the Viet Nam question is nothing but a trap for the purpose of deceiving the Soviet people and the revolutionary people of the world. . . .

You have all along been acting in coordination with the United States in its plot for peace talks, vainly attempting to sell out the struggle of the Vietnamese people against U.S. aggression and for national salvation and to drag the Viet Nam question into the orbit of Soviet-U.S. collaboration. . . .

You have even aligned yourselves with U.S. imperialism. . . . [in] a holy alliance against China, against the people, against Marxist-Leninists. . . .

We would like to inform you explicitly that since you have gone so far, the Chinese Communist party, as a serious

---

[86] *Peking Review*, No. 8, February 18, 1966, p. 10.

Marxist-Leninist party, cannot send its delegation to attend this [the 23rd Party] congress of yours. . . .

> With fraternal greetings,
> The Central Committee,
> Communist Party of China [87]

The summing up of the Chinese ideological case against the USSR appeared to come in the communique of the Central Committee of the Chinese Communist Party issued after a critical session during the upheavals associated with the Party purges and the "Great Proletarian Cultural Revolution" in the summer of 1966:

> The new leading group of the Communist Party of the Soviet Union has inherited Khrushchev's mantle and is practicing Khrushchev revisionism without Khrushchev. Their line is one of safeguarding imperialist and colonialist domination in the capitalist world and restoring capitalism in the socialist world. The leading group of the CPSU has betrayed Marxism-Leninism, betrayed the great Lenin, betrayed the road of the Great October Revolution, betrayed proletarian internationalism, betrayed the revolutionary cause of the international proletariat and of the oppressed peoples and oppressed nations, and betrayed the interests of the great Soviet people and the people of the socialist countries. . . . They are uniting with U.S.-led imperialism and the reactionaries of various countries and forming a new "Holy Alliance" against communism, the people, revolution and China. . . .
>
> The Plenary Session severely denounces the Soviet revisionist leading group for its counter-revolutionary two-faced policy of sham support but real betrayal on the question of Vietnam's resistance to U.S. aggression . . .[88]

As Soviet propaganda began to hit back, it turned Peking's charge of collusion with Washington over Vietnam against the

---

[87] Associated Press, March 24, 1966.
[88] *Peking Review*, No. 34, August 19, 1966, p. 7.

Chinese leaders themselves, and Chinese indignation mounted. Acute sensitivity to Soviet claims of tacit Chinese-American understandings on nonintervention in Vietnam was quite evident in an article distributed on February 2, 1967 by *Hsin Hua,* Peking's official news agency. Describing the Soviet charges as "barefaced lies" concocted by "the filthy swine of the Soviet revisionist leading clique," the article continued:

> This is merely another vain attempt to slander the Chinese people's just stand in resolutely supporting the Vietnamese people's struggle against U.S. aggression and to undermine the growing friendship between the Chinese and Vietnamese peoples and sabotage the heroic Vietnamese people's struggle.[89]

One can infer from this article Communist China's concern over reports of Hanoi's greater willingness to negotiate, as well as Peking's strong conviction that the Soviet Union is responsible for this slightly more flexible attitude in Hanoi.

Although Hanoi has profited in arms and other aid from both sides as a result of the Sino-Soviet competition, the intensification of the dispute has placed Ho Chi Minh and his colleagues in a somewhat awkward position. They have carefully and skillfully walked the fence during the quarrel, but this is becoming an increasingly difficult game. The *Lao Dong* Party was present at the Soviet Party Congress in March 1966, but its spokesmen were singing praises of Mao's "cultural revolution" a few months later. Hanoi knows full well that as long as the USSR ardently desires influence in North Vietnam it will continue to render both military and diplomatic support in the manner preferred by the Vietnamese Communists. However, as the behavior of the Chinese giant on the northern doorstep

---

[89] *The New York Times,* February 3, 1967, p. 3.

cannot be gauged quite so confidently, the anxiety of the Hanoi leadership can well be imagined.

The frenzied excesses of China's "Great Proletarian Cultural Revolution" and Red Guard movement have seemed to bring Moscow-Peking relations to the breaking point. We do not know to what extent the frustration of Chinese ambitions in Vietnam and Southeast Asia by American power has been a factor in the development of the recent debilitating purges and upheavals within China, but it appears that the further sundering of the world Communist movement since 1964 has been hastened by the progress of events in Vietnam.

VI

The Soviet View:
Hazards and Opportunities

In Vietnam, the Soviets have been less cautious than in Korea but more prudent than in Cuba. In the case of the Korean war, Moscow attempted to project an image of non-involvement while at the same time supplying the North Koreans and the Chinese Communists with aircraft and other military equipment and support. In the Cuban missile crisis, as we know, the Kremlin boldly played its game to the untenable extent of placing in Cuba Russian missiles capable of hitting targets in the United States.

Both in words and deeds Moscow clearly supports Hanoi, but apparently hopes to see the Vietnam War develop favorably without the hazards of a sharp and direct confrontation with the United States. The deeds include providing North Vietnam with a great number of anti-aircraft guns, surface-to-air missiles (SAMs), as well as fighter aircraft, including a number of the newer MIG-21s. Some North Vietnamese are thought to be in the Soviet Union for pilot training. How many Soviet technicians may be in North Vietnam is not known.

Despite Peking charges of Soviet collusion with the United States, Moscow has shown little inclination to help end the conflict. Quite to the contrary, the Kremlin's consistent support of Hanoi and repeated attacks on "U.S. imperialism" in

Vietnam emerge from the pages of almost every Soviet pronouncement on the subject.

There are, of course, those who argue that a greater show of "reasonableness" on the part of the United States, involving the permanent cessation of bombing the North, would result in a Soviet willingness to help end the conflict.

No doubt the Soviet Union sees Vietnam both as an opportunity and a dilemma. An opportunity exists to improve its position with the one ruling Communist Party in Southeast Asia, at the expense of the Chinese. Moreover, Moscow perhaps sees this as a chance to score an important point against China by calling for the unity of world Communism in support of Hanoi. Most of all, Moscow must find it very gratifying to see the United States directly committed to what many regard as an "unpopular war" and a hopeless struggle.

Although the USSR was at the time rather inactive in Southeast Asian affairs, it pledged support in early 1964 for the Viet Cong in their fight against American-advised South Vietnamese troops, as reported by Tass:

> True to the policy of solidarity with the peoples who are fighting for freedom and independence, they [the Soviet people] follow with profound sympathy the just national liberation struggle of the South Vietnamese people and will render the necessary assistance and support to this struggle.
> . . .
> The responsibility for the situation obtaining in South Vietnam rests above all with the United States which, flagrantly violating its obligations under the Geneva (Indochina) agreements of 1954, sent its forces to South Vietnam and unleashed an aggressive war against the South Vietnam people.[90]

In the months following Premier Kosygin's visit to Hanoi in January 1965, several ranking North Vietnamese delegations

---

[90] Associated Press, February 26, 1964.

went to Moscow to negotiate implementation of the pledge of assistance given by the Soviet leader. The following joint declaration came out of one such visit by Le Duan of the *Lao Dong* Politburo in April 1965:

> The Central Committee of the CPSU, the Soviet government, the entire Soviet people are expressing fraternal solidarity with the people of Vietnam who are waging a heroic, just struggle against the American aggressors. . . .
>
> . . . The fraternal support of the USSR and other socialist countries strengthens the Vietnamese people's faith in the ultimate victory of their just cause.
>
> The party and government delegation of the Democratic Republic of Vietnam express the profound gratitude of the Vietnamese people, the Vietnamese Workers Party and the government of the Democratic Republic of Vietnam to the fraternal Soviet people, the CPSU and the government of the USSR for the great fraternal international support and assistance. . . .
>
> The CPSU Central Committee, the Soviet government, the Central Committee of the Vietnamese Workers Party, and the government of the Democratic Republic of Vietnam reached an understanding on further steps designed to safeguard the security and defend the sovereignty of the Democratic Republic of Vietnam which is an objective of aggressive actions by American imperialism, and agreed on appropriate measures for these purposes. The Soviet Union reaffirmed its readiness to continue rendering the necessary assistance to the Democratic Republic of Vietnam for the repulsion of United States aggression. . . .[91]

The communique issued after Aleksandr Shelepin's visit to Hanoi in January 1966 contained a note of vagueness regarding the Soviet aid commitment and Soviet-Vietnamese party rela-

---

[91] Associated Press, April 18, 1965.

tions in terms of the split with Peking. It also hinted at some Soviet concern over Hanoi's inflexibility in pursuing the war:

> The Soviet delegation was deeply impressed by the enthusiasm of the working people of the Democratic Republic of Vietnam in the building of socialism, the invincible steadfastness and courage of the Vietnamese people in the struggle against the aggression of the American imperialists and for peace, independence, sovereignty, unity and the territorial integrity of their homeland, and [by] their unshakable conviction in the justice of their cause and its ultimate victory.

> The USSR and DRV delegations exchanged views on the serious situation created by the expansion by the American imperialists of the aggressive war in Vietnam and Southeast Asia and discussed certain questions of Soviet-Vietnamese relations, the international situation and a number of other questions of interest to the Soviet Union and the Democratic Republic of Vietnam.

> On behalf of the Soviet people, the Communist Party of the Soviet Union and the USSR government, the Soviet delegation declared full support for the just struggle of the Vietnamese people against the aggression by American imperialism, full support for the four points of the government of the Democratic Republic of Vietnam and the position of the National Liberation Front of South Vietnam, the sole legitimate representative of the South Vietnamese people, outlined in its statement of March 22, 1965. These positions are the only correct basis for resolving the Vietnam problem; they fully conform to the 1954 Geneva Agreements on Vietnam and meet the interests of lasting peace in Indochina and Southeast Asia. . . .

> The sides expressed satisfaction at the successful development of friendly relations between the CPSU and the WPV and between the USSR and the DRV; they discussed measures for further strengthening fraternal ties between the two parties and countries, and also examined specific

questions connected with further aid from the Soviet Union to the Democratic Republic in developing its economy, strengthening its defense capacity and repulsing the aggression of the American imperialists. . . .[92]

The summer of 1966 saw the appearance of the Warsaw Pact declaration on Vietnam which, in addition to "warning" the United States and promising Hanoi additional assistance, added the possibility that the Pact members might "allow volunteers" to join the fight in Vietnam. It will be remembered that the same threat was made by Moscow during the Egypt-Israel clash of 1956, but no "volunteers" materialized.

Having discussed the situation in Vietnam, arising from the expansion of hostilities by the United States, the parties to the Warsaw Pact:

1—Warn the Government of the United States most resolutely about the responsibility it assumes before mankind by continuing and expanding this war, for all the unforeseeable consequences that arise from this for the United States itself, among others.

2—Are rendering and will go on giving the DRV ever-increasing moral-political support and every kind of assistance, including economic help and assistance, with means of defense, materials, equipment and specialists, needed to repulse the American aggression victoriously, with due account for the requirements of the new phase of war in Vietnam.

3—Declare their readiness, if the Government of the DRV requests, to allow their volunteers to go to Vietnam in order to help the Vietnamese people in their struggle against the American aggressors.

The parties and governments of our countries believe that united actions of the socialist countries are needed to achieve the victory of the Vietnamese people. Each of our countries is resolved not to stint efforts in the future, too,

---

[92] *Pravda,* January 15, 1966, pp. 1-2.

and to take every necessary measure to help the Vietnamese people cut short the American aggression. . . .[93]

Moscow Views Vietnam and World Communist Unity

After Khrushchev's downfall, the USSR made certain efforts to soft-pedal the Sino-Soviet quarrel. In an obvious attempt to reassure Peking and convince the United States that the Soviet Union did not intend to renounce its "treaty of friendship" with Communist China, an editorial in *Pravda* in the spring of 1966 exuded friendship, cooperation and support. While admitting that "unfortunately, in the past few years difficulties between the two powers have arisen," the Moscow editorial quickly adds, "not through the fault of the Soviet side."

The editorial traces the history of earlier Sino-Soviet cooperation and wistfully speaks of the desirability of a restoration of amity through coordinated effort to aid "the Vietnamese peoples in their struggle against American aggression":

> Today is the 16th anniversary of the Treaty of Friendship, Alliance and Mutual Aid between the Soviet Union and the Chinese People's Republic.
>
> The attitude of the Soviet people toward the Chinese people has always been a model of genuine internationalism. From the very first days of the establishment of Soviet power, our country rendered the working people of China material, moral and other support in their national liberation and revolutionary struggle.
>
> Progressive people in China profoundly understood the historic significance of the alliance with the Land of Soviets for the destiny of the Chinese liberation movement . . .
>
> Unfortunately, in the past few years difficulties have arisen, not through the fault of the Soviet side, in Soviet-

---

[93] TASS, July 7, 1966.

Chinese relations. The CPSU Central Committee and the Soviet government have exerted and are exerting great efforts to overcome these difficulties and to normalize relations with the CPC and the Chinese People's Republic . . .

. . . The CPSU Central Committee and the Soviet government have repeatedly made proposals for the unification of efforts in the cause of assisting the Vietnamese people in their sacred struggle against American aggression. Any initiative by other socialist countries in this direction finds support from the Soviet side . . .

In marking the anniversary of the Soviet-Chinese treaty, the working people of our country send warm greetings to the fraternal Chinese people and express the profound conviction that the lofty principles of socialist internationalism embodied in the treaty will triumph and that relations between our countries will return to their former tested path of sincere friendship and all-around cooperation.[94]

In declining Moscow's invitation to the 23rd Soviet Party Congress in the spring of 1966, the Chinese Communists laid bare more of the nature and extent of Sino-Soviet disaffection. Peking Radio, addressing itself to the Soviet leadership said: "You sent an anti-Chinese letter to other Parties . . . inciting them to join you in opposing China. You . . . vilified the Chinese Party as being 'bellicose,' 'pseudo-revolutionary' . . . encouraging U.S. imperialist aggression, guilty of 'adventurism,' 'splittism,' 'Trotskyism,' 'nationalism,' 'great-power chauvinism' and 'dogmatism . . .' "

"In these circumstances" Peking concluded, "how can the Chinese Communist Party which you look on as an enemy, be expected to attend your congress?"

A partial text of the alleged letter mentioned in the above Chinese statement was published in the West German daily

---

[94] *Pravda*, February 14, 1966, p. 3.

Die Welt (Hamburg) on March 21, 1966. Moscow has neither confirmed nor denied the existence of such a letter:

> The Chinese people are made to believe the Soviet Union is their main enemy.
>
> . . . the Chinese side is provoking border conflicts.
>
> . . . the Chinese leaders are directing their foreign policy not so much against imperialist states as against the Soviet Union. . . .
>
> . . . the Chinese leaders have set up fractional groups in about 30 countries [and are] . . . openly interfering with the domestic affairs of other Communist parties.
>
> The course toward socialist revolution . . . has been replaced by the course toward a world war. . . .

In his opening address to the 23rd Congress of the CPSU in March 1966, Leonid Brezhnev, Soviet Communist Party First Secretary, saw Vietnam as a key to the unity (or disunity) of the world Communist movement:

> Comrades:
>
> Cooperation and solidarity is one of the main sources of strength of the socialist system. Development and deepening of this cooperation meets the vital interests of each country separately and of the world socialist system as a whole, helps rally our ranks in the struggle against imperialism.
>
> This unity is especially necessary in the present situation when American imperialists, extending their aggression against the Vietnamese people, have undertaken a brazen attack on a socialist country, the Democratic Republic of Vietnam.
>
> The CPSU has been consistently advocating the rallying of the efforts of all Socialist countries to provide assistance to fighting Vietnam. . . .

. . . we have to note at the same time, Comrades, that our relations with the parties of two socialist countries —the Chinese Communist Party and the Albanian Labor Party—unfortunately remain unsatisfactory.

Our party and the Soviet people sincerely want friendship with People's China and its Communist Party. We are prepared to do everything possible also to improve the relations with People's Albania, with the Albanian Labor Party. . . .

We still believe that such a meeting would be useful and are ready at any moment jointly with the leadership of the Chinese Communist Party to reexamine the existing differences with the object of finding ways of overcoming them on the basis of the principles of Marxism-Leninism.

We are convinced that in the long run our parties, our peoples will overcome all difficulties and will march shoulder to shoulder in the struggle for the common great revolutionary cause. . . .[95]

A July 1966 TASS "refutation" of Washington "slander" is significant as more than an example of Sino-Soviet polemics. In speaking of Washington "lies" and "criminal U.S. aggression in Vietnam," and "a bandit war against the Vietnamese people," the item casts further demonstrable doubt on the argument, tenuous at best, that Moscow really wishes to cooperate with the United States, etc., etc., on the issue of Vietnam. Moreover, the Peking charge of a "plot between the U.S. and the Soviet Union" with respect to Vietnam is rejected by the Kremlin out of hand:

Some American officials are spreading a statement that the Soviet Union allegedly was informed in advance about the bombing of areas near Hanoi and Haiphong.

TASS has been authorized to refute this lie which has been concocted in order to distort the clear position of the

---

[95] *The New York Times,* March 30, 1966.

Soviet Union in respect to the criminal U.S. aggression in Vietnam. One would think that there would be hardly anyone in his right senses who would believe such a lie. But, regretfully, it was eagerly picked up by Peking. The Vice-Premier of the State Council and the Minister of Foreign Affairs of the CPR (Chen Yi) announced at a meeting in Peking on July 10 of this year that "the bombings by the American imperialists on Hanoi and Haiphong are fully the result of a plot between the U.S. and the Soviet Union."

An impression has been gained that the lie was fabricated in Washington specifically in the hope that it would be picked up by politicians in Peking who are susceptible to anti-Soviet falsifications. With this new slander on the Soviet Union, in unison with the fabrications of American propaganda, Chen Yi is actually serving the cause of the U.S. imperialists who are leading a bandit war against the Vietnamese people.[96]

In a statement to the Supreme Soviet on August 3, 1966, Premier Kosygin put to rest any suggestion that with the political demise of Khrushchev, the Sino-Soviet dispute could be patched up. He said that Peking, by attacking the Soviet Union, "renders a big service to the American imperialists."

The positions of the Socialist community in the world arena would have been even stronger had there been unity and all-around cooperation also with the Chinese People's Republic. Unfortunately all our attempts to improve relations with the CPR remain without result.

The Chinese leaders and the Chinese press are systematically coming out against the CPSU and the USSR. These attacks distort the essence of our party's and state's course and have nothing in common with reality. Continuing to speak about struggle against imperialism, the Chinese propaganda, especially in recent times, is increas-

---

[96] *Pravda*, July 15, 1966, p. 4.

ingly making the CPSU and the Soviet Union the main target of its attacks and thereby, as it is obvious to everybody, renders a big service to the American imperialists.

The CPSU Central Committee and the Soviet Government are convinced that the tensions existing in Soviet-Chinese relations contradict the nature of Socialist relations inside the world system of Socialism.

In its policy in respect of the CPR, the Soviet Government will continue to proceed from the sincere striving of our party and people to restore friendly relations and unity with People's China on the principal basis of Marxism-Leninism and proletarian internationalism. This position meets the interests of Socialist countries, including the interests of the Chinese people itself, the interests of the general struggle against imperialism, for peace and social progress.[97]

By early 1967, as Moscow-Peking diplomatic relations seemed to be approaching a formal break, the Soviets were publicly reporting in specifics about Chinese interference with Russian aid crossing China en route to Hanoi. After Soviet diplomatic sources alleged Chinese "highjacking" of air defense missiles, the government paper *Izvestia* reported interference at Peking airport with Soviet aircraft and technicians proceeding to North Vietnam:

A most disgusting provocation by the Chinese occurred at the Peking airport on January 31, when Soviet planes made a stopover en route to Vietnam. A mass of demonstrators gathered, shouting anti-Soviet slogans, chanting quotations from the works of Mao Tse-tung, and maliciously insulting the Soviet people.

The passengers aboard the planes—Soviet specialists going to Vietnam to help the Vietnamese people—were forced to remain aboard the craft. In violation of all normal safety

[97] *The New York Times*, August 4, 1966, p. 2.

regulations, the aircraft were compelled to refuel with the passengers aboard.

Chinese officials, under various pretexts, repeatedly delayed the take-off of the planes. Then, when the engines of one of the aircraft had already been started, the Chinese stated that it was necessary to carry out further "checking of documents." Representatives of Aeroflot were subjected to insults and humiliation. . . .[98]

By the spring of 1967, however, there were reports that Moscow and Peking had reached agreement permitting unimpeded Soviet shipment of military equipment and supplies through China to Vietnam. Whether this action represents anything more than a temporary and expedient arrangement is uncertain. At any rate, Hanoi's attitude on peace negotiations seems to have hardened, and there is conjecture that this has been due to the reported Sino-Soviet deal.

Vietnam as a Barometer of U.S.-USSR Relations

How does Moscow's much heralded policy of peaceful coexistence square with its military assistance to North Vietnam in the latter's attempt to take over South Vietnam? Peaceful coexistence as the Soviets employ the term means simply the absence of nuclear war. It does not imply the abandonment of the ideology of Marxism-Leninism nor the solution of any of the major foreign policy issues between the Soviet Union and the United States, except on Moscow's terms.

By reversing the facts on Vietnam, as in the previous cases of Communist aggression where the West has responded to defend its own interest and those of its friends, Moscow attempts to

---

[98] *Izvestia,* February 3, 1967.

paint the United States as the aggressor and therefore to lay the blame on the United States for the deterioration of Moscow's relations with Washington. Brezhnev's comments at the 23rd Congress illustrated once again the Soviet definition of true "peaceful coexistence" as the absence of Free World resistance to Communist aggression:

> Special mention must be made of the United States imperialist aggression against Vietnam. In flagrant violation of the Geneva agreements, the United States has piratically attacked the Democratic Republic of Vietnam and is waging a bloody war against the people of South Vietnam. . . .
>
> We declare categorically that in escalating the shameful war against the Vietnamese people the United States will have to contend with mounting support for Vietnam from the Soviet Union and other socialist friends and brothers. . . .
>
> In connection with United States aggression in Vietnam and other aggressive acts of American imperialism our relations with the United States have worsened. The blame for this is on the ruling quarters of the United States.
>
> The USSR is prepared to live at peace with all countries, but it will not resign itself to imperialist iniquity against other peoples. We have repeatedly declared that we are prepared to develop our relations with the United States, and stand by this position now.
>
> But this requires that the United States discontinue its policy of aggression. . . .[99]

Foreign Minister Andrei Gromyko's report to the 23rd Party Congress also underlined and elaborated the same theme. While repeating the usual clichés about "American circles that plunged their country into war against the Vietnamese people,"

---

[99] *The New York Times*, March 30, 1966.

the statement as a whole has a certain restrained tone conspicuously different from the repeated belligerent statements
out of Peking. It sounded as if the lessons of Cuba and Tonkin
Gulf, as well as the generally firm Asian policies of the United
States government in recent years, had suggested the wisdom of
caution to the policy-makers in Moscow—just as these factors
had influenced Peking's response to remain largely in the realm
of words rather than deeds:

> The contrast between the two trends of foreign policy
> —the peaceful and the aggressive—has been especially
> apparent in connection with the events in Vietnam. The
> actions of the United States of America in Vietnam con-
> stitute aggression unleashed by the greatest imperialist
> power.

> The more clearly the peoples perceive the answer offered
> by one government or another to the question of war and
> peace, the sooner they will pass sentence on the social
> system whose nature is reflected in the arms race, the
> gospel of militarism and highhandedness in international
> affairs. . . .

> How is foreign policy to be conducted when there is such
> an obvious difference, such a counterposition of basic orien-
> tations in international policies?

> Should we simply lose our tempers and slam the door, so
> to speak, wasting no time or effort on negotiation with
> the Western powers responsible for the tensions in the
> world? Or should we nevertheless raise problems that
> have become ripe and strive for their solution, relying
> on the support of all peace-loving forces, and cooperating
> with those forces in the bourgeois camp who realize how
> necessary it is to normalize international relations?

> The second approach is the only correct one and is pre-
> cisely the one consistently supported by our party's Central
> Committee and the Soviet government. . . .

Our party's Central Committee and its Presidium day by day and concretely direct the entire multifaceted activity of the Soviet state. This is precisely why the strength of Soviet foreign policy—a Leninist policy—is well known not only to our country and our friends with whom we work hand in hand but also to those whom fate has destined us to confront in the international arena. . . .

With the political course steered by the United States of America it is not at all difficult to create international crises. But in international relations there is a line that must not be crossed by any government if it is not to exchange a responsible policy for the dangerous game of all-or-nothing.[100]

In his August 3, 1966 statement to the Supreme Soviet, Kosygin went out of his way to assure the deputies of the Supreme Soviet that while aiding the Vietnamese people to "drive the Americans away . . . we shall display restraint and calmness. . . .":

The Soviet Union's relations with the capitalist countries, which we are prepared to develop on the basis of the principles of peaceful coexistence, constitute an important direction of the Soviet Union's activity in foreign policy . . .

A direct threat to general security is created by the United States aggression in Vietnam, which is beginning to spread also to Laos and Cambodia . . . A conflict has broken out which to a great extent determines the situation in the world and influences the solution of the most important international problems.

The continuation of the aggression inevitably leads to further expansion of the boundaries of the conflict . . .

I would like to assure the deputies of the Supreme Soviet of the USSR that the Soviet Government will do everything

---

[100] *Pravda,* April 3, 1966, pp. 4-5.

in its power to help the Vietnamese people to drive the American invaders away from the Vietnamese soil at the earliest possible date. . . .

At the same time we shall display restraint and calmness, and will not be taken in by the provocations of those who would like to warm their hands at the hotbeds of international tensions, at the hotbeds of war.

The Soviet Union pursues and will go on pursuing a policy of peace and peaceful coexistence of states with different social systems, a policy of easing international tension. We are ready—to the extent the others are prepared for this—to traverse our part of the road towards mutual understanding and accord among the states.[101]

Whatever the appearances of the Soviet posture on Vietnam at any given time, it is unlikely that Moscow would turn aside an opportunity for a "settlement" which could be represented as a Soviet diplomatic victory—perhaps over both the United States and Communist China. In view of some of the exaggerated claims the Maoists make for their strategy of revolutionary people's war, it would be richly ironic if a combination of Soviet heavy armaments and "revisionist" diplomacy should play a major role in a struggle inspired, organized and built by Asian Communist cadres.

---

[101] *The New York Times, op. cit.*

VII

Conclusion

Being the most dynamic of the organized revolutionary movements in post-World War II Southeast Asia, Vietnamese Communism has been the focus of international politics in that part of the world for the last two decades. The Viet Cong movement and the present Vietnam War represent the culmination of a drive to complete the occupation and organization of a base for projecting Hanoi's future ambitions. Vietnamese Communism and the Viet Cong also bear the burden of great expectations on the part of the major Communist power centers in a way that no other Asian Marxist movement does. Thus the Vietnam War has come to represent for the Communists, and particularly for Peking, the great test of revolutionary war strategy designed to outflank the West's military preponderance and to nullify its economic and technological superiority.

Traditional Soviet and Chinese Communist doctrines of revolutionary struggle have been fitted to the Vietnamese environment—in some cases very well, in others rather awkwardly. Variations of the Soviet and Chinese models of revolutionary warfare have developed, some as a natural consequence of varying conditions, others deliberate deviations tailored to different specific objectives. In some aspects, the Viet Cong differ considerably not only from Soviet and Chinese examples but also from their direct lineal predecessors, the Viet Minh.

Although Lenin formulated some early doctrine for the organization of revolutionary movements in Asia, the ambivalence of Soviet policy in the Far East and its early misdirected emphasis on labor movements and urban uprisings left the field of Asian Communist revolutionary strategy to Mao Tse-tung. As a result of this default and Mao's success in China, the Vietnamese Communists, despite their strong traditional organizational ties with Moscow, appear to derive their principal inspiration and operational guidelines from Maoist doctrine. The facts of geography and power tend to reinforce this tie, whatever the independent thrust of Vietnamese nationalism may be, and despite certain misgivings, born of history, regarding the not always benevolent Chinese neighbor to the north.

A great deal of mythology has developed in regard to the Vietnam War. As previously pointed out, this documentary study was not designed to deal with the question of American national interests in Vietnam, about which there are honest, if often uninformed, differences of opinion. However, there is no lack of documentary evidence important in understanding what has actually been happening in Vietnam—the origins of the war, the objectives of the Communist powers and the nature of the Viet Cong movement. Total documentation on these several issues will not be possible for a long time, but the bulk of what evidence is now available points clearly to certain significant conclusions.

Regardless of the extent to which the Viet Cong movement represents an indigenous social revolution in South Vietnam (all Communist revolutions are by definition social upheavals), the essential feature of the insurgency is that it represents Ho Chi Minh's attempt to destroy the non-Communist southern republic by force and thus complete the work in which he and his revolutionary colleagues have been engaged since the founding of the Indochinese Communist Party in, 1930. Hanoi has provided both the inspiration and the operational control of the Viet Cong movement from the outset. North Vietnam pursues its course with a rigidly austere determination born of confidence in its excellent political organization, in the fighting qualities of its army, and in the "immutable" laws of history and of revolutionary war, buoyed by hope that disunity and frustration in the United States will undermine the American effort. Nevertheless, the Hanoi leaders may decide to negotiate if they feel that this will advance their cause more profitably than the pursuit of armed aggression. It is extremely doubtful that a settlement reached in negotiations will be very stable or will solve the basic issues in Vietnam.

To be sure, the war in Vietnam has certain attributes of a civil conflict. At the same time, it quite clearly represents an aggression by North Vietnam, aided by the words and deeds of Communist China and the USSR, against a sovereign state in the other half of Vietnam recognized by the majority of the world's independent nations. The future at stake is that of South Vietnam. The fact remains that nearly half the Vietnamese population were developing and even prospering in a non-Marxist framework until set upon violently by their Communist compatriots. The deviousness with which this assault from the North has been carried out, compared to the direct attack by the North Koreans on their brothers in 1950, does not change the essential parallelism of the two aggressions —though it does tend to complicate and confuse the issues in Vietnam.

Although the Viet Cong have developed a vast and effective political organization and have expended great persuasive efforts through informal and formal propaganda, it would be entirely erroneous to suggest that they command the genuine allegiance of the South Vietnamese people. A significant part of the support they have received has been due to massive coercion; some of it results from pervasive psychological pressures and a large element of it from outright terror. The large-scale and persistent use of terror as a weapon and its integration and coordination with military operations are the Viet Cong's special contribution to the art of revolutionary war. But there is now some indication that this brutal campaign, along with excessive taxation and conscription, is alienating peasant support of the Viet Cong.

No significant support for the Viet Cong comes from the educated elite or the urban population. The National Liberation Front has attracted nothing but nonentities to man the "non-Communist" positions in its public facade. Excellent organization and effective operational technique do not appear to be enough to offset a "faceless" Viet Cong leadership in the South which is subservient to Hanoi and which seems unable to articulate to the elite or the masses either a credible image of an enemy or a convincing program for alleviating the ills of South Vietnamese society.

For years the Viet Cong fought a protracted war against an incumbent regime increasingly weakened by its own instability, inefficiency, and inertia, as well as by public apathy and war-weariness. By all the usual indicators, the Communists should have won before the massive military intervention of the United States. Yet the fact that all resistance did not collapse indicates that, in addition to some missing ingredient in the Viet Cong program, there has been at least a rudimentary awareness on the part of the average South Vietnamese that his present hard lot might become infinitely worse should he be swallowed up in a Communist state such as North Vietnam represents. Whatever the reasons, the will to resist the Viet Cong has been growing, as demonstrated by the increasing stability of the South Vietnamese government, the remarkable voter participation in the Constituent Assembly and village elections of 1966 and 1967, and the successful formulation of a new Constitution. At the same time, however, grave problems of pacification of the countryside still remain.

When and if the turn of the military tide also begins to undermine the Viet Cong's political foundations seriously, the Communists will be faced with crucial decisions which will determine their future as a significant force in South Vietnam. Should they decide at a suitable time to end the armed struggle and revert to a largely political conflict, they are likely to be able to maintain themselves as a serious factor in the country's life for a very long period, provided morale can be sustained. The subversive challenge they will then represent may well be as critical as their military threat since 1959.

Although Peking and Moscow have aided and abetted the Vietnamese Communists in this war, they have done so with caution and with little evident unity of purpose. Far from providing at least one common ground for cooperation, the Vietnam War has become the focal point for a decisive intensification of the Sino-Soviet dispute. However, the Soviet and Chinese leaders share a desire to see American power either removed from or hamstrung in Vietnam, but both show an eloquent prudence of action in the fact of that power.

Communist China may well have been quite confident in the 1963-64 period that the Vietnam War could be brought to a successful conclusion at an early date. However, it has been quite evident since the United States assumed full military, economic, and diplomatic roles in Vietnam that Peking now sees the war as a "protracted" struggle which should be fought to the last Vietnamese. Chinese commitments remain somewhat nebulous. A hope that the American effort will be widely dispersed and endlessly frustrated by such "people's" wars and eroded by the critics at home is inherent in the Chinese posture.

The Soviet dilemma in Vietnam continues to revolve around the extent to which the USSR can use this unique opportunity to re-establish its position in North Vietnam and score important points in its struggle with Peking without a dangerous, direct confrontation with the United States and abandonment of the profitable concept of "peaceful coexistence." Nonetheless, it is well to remember that both Moscow and Peking are providing Hanoi with economic and military assistance on an increasing scale.

With its cautious policy of fence-straddling, Hanoi has achieved an enviable position as recipient of material support from both Communist giants, but remains without a specific major commitment of direct intervention from either should decisive deterioration of the war situation occur. Much will depend, of course, on the results of the present Chinese internal upheaval and struggle for power, particularly insofar as this situation reflects the issue of caution vs. audacity in foreign policy.

The present international system seems to provide from time to time a "third arena" in which the major powers can communicate to each other their strengths, weaknesses, and intentions without direct confrontation. At a terrible price to its suffering people, Vietnam has provided such a stage. An internal war tends to become "internationalized" when it takes on real significance, even if only symbolic, for outside powers. While the danger of a greater conflagration is always present, there is at least a possibility that the Communists have been brought to a greater sense of realism through the opportunity provided by Vietnam to measure American determination. If, as a result of this appraisal, they decide that without undue risks they cannot win the present struggle by shooting, a significant round will have been won against the challenge of Communist revolutionary war strategy. This in turn should make it possible to get on with the more desirable and important task of assisting the Vietnamese people to build a more prosperous and stable society, free from chaos, hunger and Communist tyranny.

Bibliography

(IN ORDER OF APPEARANCE IN TEXT)

V. I. Lenin, *The National Liberation Movement in the East.* (Moscow: Foreign Languages Publishing House, 1957).

N. S. Khrushchev, "For New Victories of the World Communist Movement." *Pravda,* January 25, 1961.

Thomas W. Wolfe, *Soviet Strategy at the Crossroads.* (Cambridge: Harvard University Press, 1964).

V. D. Sokolovsky, *Soviet Military Strategy.* (Englewood Cliffs: Prentice-Hall, 1963).

Douglas Pike, "How Strong Is the NLF?". *The Reporter,* February 24, 1966.

Stuart R. Schram, "The Military Deviation of Mao Tse-tung." *Problems of Communism,* January-February 1964.

Mao Tse-tung, *Selected Military Writings.* (Peking: Foreign Languages Press, 1963).

Tang Tsou and Morton Halperin, "Maoism at Home and Abroad." *Problems of Communism,* July-August 1965.

Vo Nguyen Giap, *People's War, People's Army.* American Edition. (New York: Frederick Praeger, 1962).

Lin Piao, "Long Live the Victory of People's War!" *Peking Review,* No. 36, September 3, 1965.

Resolutions and Speeches at the Third National Congress of the *Lao Dong* (Workers) Party of Vietnam in Hanoi, September, 1960, in *A Threat to the Peace.* (Washington, D.C.: U.S. Government Printing Office, 1961).

Truong Chinh on the Revolution in the South. *Hoc Tap,* Hanoi, April 1961.

Department of State, *Aggression from the North.* (Washington, D.C.: U.S. Government Printing Office, 1965).

Article on the NLF as a "Cleverly Applied" Tactic. *Hoc Tap,* September 1966.

Editorial on the 37th Anniversary of the *Lao Dong. Liberation Army,* February 2, 1967.

Pham Van Dong, Interview with Aptheker and Lynd. *Vietnam News Agency,* January 28, 1961.

Truong Chinh, Interview on Vanguard Role of the Party. *Vietnam News Agency,* January 11, 1967.

Nhan Dan (The People), Hanoi, Editorial on the Viet Cong, April 9, 1965.

Ho Chi Minh, Interview with Felix Greene, *Vietnam Courier,* No. 42, December 16, 1965.

Ho Chi Minh, Letter to the Chiefs of State of Socialist Countries. *Vietnam News Agency,* January 28, 1966.

Foreign Office, "Documents Relating to British Involvement in the Indo-China Conflict, 1945-1965." Cmnd. 2834. (London: Her Majesty's Stationery Office, 1965).

National Assembly of the Democratic Republic of Vietnam, Hanoi, Resolution on the Four Conditions Necessary to Peace in Vietnam. *Vietnam News Agency,* April 13, 1965.

Hanoi Radio Commentary on the National Liberation Front as the Sole Representative of the South Vietnamese People, January 27, 1966.

Foreign Office, "Recent Exchanges Concerning Attempts to Promote a Negotiated Settlement of the Conflict in Vietnam." Cmnd. 2756. (London: Her Majesty's Stationery Office, 1965).

Ho Chi Minh, "Reply to Pope Paul." *The New York Times,* December 30, 1965.

Foreign Ministry, Hanoi, Rejection of U.N. Role in Vietnam War. *Vietnam News Agency,* February 1, 1966.

Pham Van Dong, Statement to Harrison Salisbury. *The New York Times,* January 8, 1965.

Pham Van Dong, Report to the National Assembly, Hanoi Radio, April 13, 1965.

Vo Nguyen Giap, "Our People Will Surely Defeat the U.S. Aggressors." *Hoc Tap,* Hanoi, January 1966.

Le Duc Tho, "Let Us Change the Trend and Step Up the Party Building Task in Order to Insure Successful Carrying Out of the Anti-U.S. Struggle for National Salvation." *Hoc Tap,* Hanoi, February 1966.

Ho Chi Minh, "Fight until Complete Victory!", Hanoi Radio, July 17, 1966.

Hanoi Radio, Reports of Conferences of Security Forces and Political Dept. of Transportation Service, September 12 and October 22, 1966.

Justus M. Van der Kroef, "The War Seen from Hanoi." *Vietnam Perspectives,* Vol. 1, No. 3, February 1966.

Souvanna Phouma, Address on Laotian Armed Forces Day, March 23, 1966.

Hammond M. Rolph, "The Viet Cong: Politics at Gunpoint." *Communist Affairs,* Vol. 4, No. 4, July-August 1966.

Bernard Fall, *The Two Viet-Nams.* (New York: Praeger, 1964).

National Front for Liberation of South Vietnam, "Resist to the End, Until the Last U.S. Aggressor is Driven out of Vietnam." *Hsin Hua News Agency,* Hong Kong, *Selected News Items,* June 1965.

Douglas Pike, *Viet Cong.* (Cambridge: M.I.T. Press, 1966).

U.S. Mission in Vietnam, *The Communist Party of South Vietnam—A Study.* Saigon, March 1966.

Captured Viet Cong Document, "Rules for the [Communist] Party in South Vietnam." Undated. Acquired 1965.

George Carver, "The Faceless Viet Cong." *Foreign Affairs,* April 1966.

"Women of South Vietnam." *Intersol,* Hanoi, August 1965.

Takashi Oka, "The Other Regime in South Vietnam." *The New York Times Magazine,* July 31, 1966.

Captured Viet Cong Document, "Women's Movement for Establishment of the 'Glorious Family.' " Acquired late 1965.

Captured Viet Cong Document, "Rural Support Policy." Dated 1965. Acquired mid-1965.

Captured Viet Cong Document, "Policy of the NLF toward Officers and Men of the Republic of Vietnam Armed Forces." Acquired August 1965.

Captured Viet Cong Document, "Future Propaganda and Indoctrination Tasks in Towns." Acquired October 1965.

Captured Viet Cong Document, "Policy of the NLF toward the Ethnic Minorities of South Vietnam." Dated August 1962.

Viet Cong Extortion Letter Sent to Saigon Area Businessmen. Acquired 1965.

U.S. Mission in Vietnam, *Viet Cong Use of Terror—A Study.* Saigon, May 1966.

Captured Viet Cong Directive on Assassinations, Acquired in "D" Zone, January 1966.

Joint U.S. Public Affairs Office, Vietnam, "Review of Current Viet Cong Propaganda Efforts." Field Memo No. 2, September 30, 1965.

Viet Cong Propaganda Leaflet, "Letter to Officers and Non-Coms in Positions Encircled by Our Forces." Captured September 1965.

Untitled 1964 Viet Cong Propaganda Leaflet addressed to "Officers and Soldiers in the Southern Army."

Viet Cong Propaganda Leaflet, "Do Not Kill, Burn and Rob the People!" Addressed to ARVN personnel. Dated 1962.

Viet Cong Propaganda Leaflet, "Countering the Strategic Hamlet Plan of US-Diem." Dated April 1961.

Viet Cong Propaganda Leaflet, "Summons of the Labor Liberation Front in Saigon on May Day." Dated May 1, 1965.

Miscellaneous Viet Cong English-language slogan slips directed to U.S. servicemen. Acquired early 1966.

Captured Viet Cong Document, "Report on Propaganda and Foreign Affairs." Acquired March 1967.

Nguyen Huu Tho, "Speech on the 5th Anniversary of the NLF." Hanoi: *Vietnam News Agency,* December 21, 1965.

Nguyen Huu Tho, Interview with Wilfred Burchett. Liberation Radio, September 13, 1966.

Captured Viet Cong Document, Letter to Party Cadres Regarding Training and Morale, dated December 15, 1965.

Editorial on Cadre Moral. *Tien Phong,* January 1966.

Liberation Radio (Clandestine) Commentary on September 1966 South Vietnamese Elections, "Shameful Failure of a Fraud." September 12, 1966.

Captured Viet Cong Document, "Counter 'Open Arms' Activities," Acquired April 1967.

Editorial. "Develop the Success of the Second All-Southern Political Conference . . . " *Quan Giai Phong,* September 18, 1966.

Speech by North Vietnamese Gen. Nguyen Van Vinh at Fourth COSVN Congress. Text captured April 1967.

Statement of the Government of the People's Republic of China, "U.S. Aggression against Viet Nam Democratic Republic Means Aggression against China." *Peking Review* No. 32, August 7, 1964.

Chen Yi, "Aiding Viet Nam Is China's Sacred Internationalist Duty." *Peking Review* No. 14, April 2, 1965.

Resolution of the Standing Committee, National People's Congress of China, "Resolute and Unreserved Support for Viet Nam." *Peking Review* No. 17, April 23, 1965.

Chou En-lai, "China Is Ready to Take Up U.S. Challenge." *Peking Review* No. 52, December 24, 1965.

Liu Shao-chi, "China Resolutely Supports DRV's Just Stand." *Peking Review* No. 6, February 4, 1966.

Liu Shao-chi, Speech in Honor of Kwame Nkrumah. *Peking Review* No. 10, March 4, 1966.

Editorial, "The 700 Million Chinese People Pledge to Back the Vietnamese People." Peking: *Jen Min Jih Pao,* July 18, 1966.

Editorial, "The Broad Masses of American People Undergo a Profound Revolutionary Change." *Jen Min Jih Pao,* February 7, 1966.

Editorial, "World Upheavals Are Good for Revolutionaries." *Jen Min Jih Pao,* March 1, 1966.

Editorial on "Ebbs and Flows in the Movement of the People." *Jen Min Jih Pao,* March 9, 1966.

"USSR Refuses to Clear Up Anti-China Rumours." *Hsin Hua News Agency,* January 15, 1966.

Editorial, "Confessions Concerning the Line of Soviet-U.S. Collaboration Pursued by the New Leaders of the CPSU." *Hung Ch'i* No. 2, February 11, 1966.

Letter from Central Committee, Communist Party of China, to Central Committee, Communist Party of the Soviet Union, rejecting invitation to 23rd Congress of the CPSU.

Communique of the Eleventh Plenary Session of the Eighth Central Committee of the Communist Party of China, Adopted August 12, 1966. *Peking Review* No. 34, August 19, 1966.

Article Refuting Soviet Claims of US-Chinese Understanding. *Hsin Hua,* February 2, 1967.

USSR Statement of Support for the Viet Cong. Moscow: TASS, April 18, 1965.

USSR-DRV Joint Communique on the Vietnam War, TASS, April 18, 1965.

USSR-DRV Joint Communique on Visit to Hanoi by A. N. Shelepin. *Pravda,* January 15, 1966.

Central Committee, Communist Party of the Soviet Union, Secret Anti-China Circular Letter. Hamburg: *Die Welt.* (Extracts in *Communist Affairs,* Vol. 4 No. 2, March-April 1966.)

Leonid Brezhnev, Opening Address to the 23rd Congress, CPSU. *The New York Times,* March 30, 1966.

"Refutation of Chinese Slander by TASS." *Pravda,* July 15, 1966.

Article on Chinese Interference with Soviet Flights to Vietnam. *Izvestia,* February 3, 1967.

Aleksei N. Kosygin, Statement to the Meeting of the Supreme Soviet. *The New York Times,* August 4, 1966.

Andrei Gromyko, Report on Foreign Affairs to the 23rd Congress, CPSU. *Pravda,* April 3, 1966.